Wm. Cebie Smith

Wm. Cebie Smith

San

Lane Magazine & Book Company

Francisco

A Sunset Pictorial

Menlo Park, California

San Francisco

by the EDITORS of SUNSET BOOKS and SUNSET MAGAZINE

EDITED BY JACK McDOWELL

DESIGN AND GRAPHICS COORDINATION: William Gibson, Joe Seney

CARTOGRAPHY: Phillip Willette

ILLUSTRATIONS: Gordon Brusstar

EDITORIAL ASSISTANTS: Elizabeth Hogan, Mary Benton Smith

SPECIAL CONSULTANTS: George Knight, American Society of
Magazine Photographers
Richard Dillon, Sutro Library

PHOTOGRAPHS

ANSEL ADAMS: 17; 42 (all courtesy REDWOOD EMPIRE ASSOCIATION). AIR-PHOTO, INC.: 270. BANCROFT LIBRARY, UNIVERSITY OF CALIFORNIA, BERKELEY: 19; 21 lower; 23 lower; 27; 34 upper; 35. BANK OF AMERICA: 153 lower far right. BAY AREA RAPID TRANSIT: 258; 262; 263; 264. LEE BLODGET: 8; 9; 11; 72; 159 right; 196. RICHARD BROOKS: 167; 177 right. MICHAEL BRY: 79 upper; 85; 97 upper; 110 upper; 114 upper right; 123 upper; 126 upper right; 146; 156 lower; 171 lower; 182 right; 189. CALIFORNIA HISTORICAL SOCIETY: 29; 37. NICK CARTER: 10; 220 upper; 236. WILLIAM CARTER: 93 right; 96; 105; 108; 124; 125; 128; 194; 248; 254. GLENN CHRISTIANSEN: 76 lower; 80; 81 upper right; 134; 161; 199; 200; 213 upper; 216 right; 218; 247 upper; 271 left. ANNA-JEAN COLE: 114 upper left; 208. FRAN COLEBERD: 18; 104 right; 118 upper; 144; 195 lower; 247 lower. ROBERT COX: 133. MADISON DEVLIN: 47; 102; 178; 180; 190; 235; 261 upper. J. R. EYERMAN: 70. RANDOLPH FALK: 170. GEORGE FITZGERALD: 187 lower. JOSHUA FREIWALD: 223 upper right. GOLDEN GATE BRIDGE: 240 upper. DAVE HARTLEY: 191. MIKE HAYDEN: 193 upper. EDWIN HOFFMAN: 50 lower; 88 upper. BOB HOLLINGSWORTH: 107 upper; 110 lower; 111 upper; 121; 140; 206 left; 207 right; 228; 229; 230. INTERNATIONAL MARKET CENTER: 268 left. ROBERT ISAACS: 82 upper right; 127; 132; 188 lower; 233; 243. PIRKLE JONES: 129 lower. CURT W. KALDOR: 2-3. GEORGE KNIGHT: Front Cover; 38 upper; 81 lower; 88 lower left, lower right; 91; 95; 99; 103; 122; 145; 151; 168 upper; 174 lower; 246 upper; 253; 259. HOLGER KREUZHAGE: 183. JOHN LARSEN: 77; 185; 226 left; 272. LIBRARY OF CONGRESS: 21 upper. ELLS MARUGG: 148 lower; 149; 152; 271 right. ELAINE MAYES: 147 upper. MIKE McCURRY: 97 lower; 123 lower; 142 right; 163; 206 right; 207 left; 266. JACK McDOWELL: 6-7; 25; 26; 81 upper left; 88 lower center; 100 lower; 109 lower; 111 lower; 112; 115; 116 right; 118 lower; 119 left; 130 upper; 131; 141 upper right; 142 left; 143 upper right; 147 lower; 159 left; 164 left; 165 lower right; 186; 188 upper; 193 lower; 201; 203 right; 205; 209; 211 lower; 212; 213 lower; 215 upper; 217; 224; 239; 245 center, right; 255; 256; 257; 260; 261 lower; 267 upper. WILLIAM McKINNEY: 172. PHIZ MOZESSON: 109 upper. DAVID MUENCH: 106 lower; 154-155. TOM MYERS: 71; 93 left; 129; 162; 214 upper. PATRICK O'ROURKE: 62. PACIFIC GAS & ELECTRIC: 220 lower; 222; 223 lower. PHIL PALMER: 69; 98; 104 left; 137; 157; 181. RODOLFO PETSCHEK: 160. PIONEER SOCIETY OF CALIFORNIA: 20; 23 upper; 30 lower; 33; 34 lower; 41; 45; 55. BIL PLUMMER: 76 lower; 78 lower; 79 lower; 82 left, lower right; 94; 101; 116 left; 117; 153 upper; 174 upper; 175 upper; 176; 179; 214 lower; 246 lower; 249. WALLACE PONTIUS: 221 upper. REDWOOD EMPIRE ASSOCIATION: 22; 83; 143 left; 242. KARL RIEK: 148 upper. MARTHA ROSMAN: 78 upper; 130 lower. HAL ROTH: 92; 119 center. SAN FRANCISCO CHAMBER OF COMMERCE: 61; 216 left; 269 right. SAN FRANCISCO CONVENTION & VISITORS BUREAU: 177 left; 182 left; 197; 198; 210; 225 right; 234; 238. SAN FRANCISCO EXAMINER: 74. SAN FRANCISCO PORT AUTHORITY: 156 upper. SAN FRANCISCO PRESIDIO: 30 upper; 31 lower. SAN FRANCISCO PUBLIC UTILITIES COMMISSION: 244; 245 lower left. SAN FRANCISCO REDEVELOPMENT AGENCY: 267 lower; 269 left. SAN FRANCISCO WARRIORS: 195 upper. SHERATON-PALACE HOTEL: 60. SMITHSONIAN INSTITUTION: 38 lower; 48; 51. SOUTHERN PACIFIC: 46 upper; 53; 54 upper; 56 left, right; 57; 58; 59 lower left, lower center left, lower right; 107 lower. LEVI STRAUSS & CO.: 49. TOM TRACY: 87. TEDDY TSOI: 90 lower left, lower right; 126 upper left, lower; 221 lower. UNION PACIFIC RAILROAD MUSEUM COLLECTION: 56 center. U. S. ARMY SIGNAL CORPS: 223 upper center. McLEOD VOLZ: 114 lower. CHARLES WECKLER: Back Cover. WELLS FARGO BANK HISTORY ROOM: 36; 39; 40; 43; 46 lower; 50 upper; 52; 54 lower left, lower left center, lower center right, lower right; 59 upper, lower center right; 63; 153 lower left, lower center left, lower center right; 173; 187 upper; 203 left. BARON WOLMAN: 139; 171 lower. GEORGE WOO: 90 upper; 135; 164 right; 165 left, upper right; 237. YORK SECURITIES: 268 right. NATHAN ZABARSKY: 241. NIKOLAY ZUREK: 31 upper; 100 upper; 106 upper; 113; 138; 141 upper left, lower; 143 lower right, center right; 168 lower; 169; 175 lower; 192; 211 upper; 219; 225 left; 226 upper right, center right, lower right.

Executive Editor, Sunset Books: David E. Clark

Contents

San Francisco—a peninsular city, formed through the forces of

a capricious sea, a restless bay, and a benevolent climate.

7

A clean, white city, shaped by the timeless energies of nature and the tireless exuberance of man—a city whose independent spirit is fostered by its physical isolation, whose variety derives from the character of the people attracted to its shores.

A compact city, whose structures thrust boldly toward the clouds, whose residents respect the past and savor the present while stepping with unhurried confidence toward the future.

11

The city's cradle days were calm, quiet—and relatively short-lived. With the discovery of gold, San Francisco entered its brawling youth. By the time of the silver boom, some of the rough edges were beginning to wear off. But only after its partial destruction did the city settle down to maturity and honest self-respect.

BEGINNINGS OF A BOOM TOWN

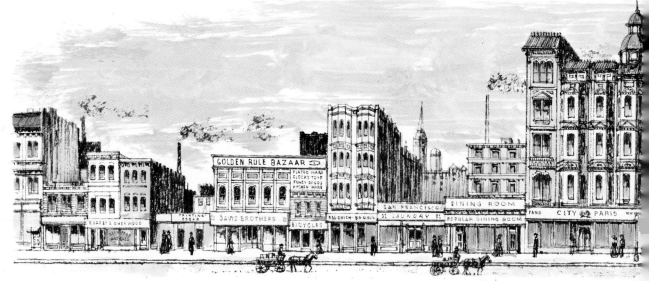

Retail row, about 1894—Geary Street, between Kearny and Stockton.

THE DISCOVERY of what today is San Francisco was an ironic accident, a twist of fate that started a pattern of fitful boom and bust that characterized the place for decades to follow.

By the middle of the eighteenth century, Spanish treasure galleons and ships of exploration had been voyaging up and down the California coast for well over two hundred years. The mariners were prudent enough to stay well off the unknown and rugged shoreline, but in so doing they time and time again sailed past a narrow inlet beyond which lay a gigantic natural harbor. In 1769 a land expedition led by Don Gaspar de Portola was sent out from Mexico to extend Spanish colonization in what seemed a territory of great promise—Alta California. The party's target was Monterey, where a settlement had already been established, and on the way north it kept near the coast except when forced by mountains or other natural obstacles to turn inland. One such barrier caused the expedition to detour shortly before it would have reached Monterey. Several days later the travel-weary Portola found his way blocked by a large and unidentifiable body of water—the bay of San Francisco. Rather than feeling any proprietary right in the discovery, Portola was bitterly disappointed at having missed his objective.

By the late 1700's Spain was becoming increasingly concerned over the possibility of Russia putting colonists into California, and the Viceroy at Mexico City sent the ship *San Carlos* north, instructing Captain Manuel de

Yerba Buena...a forgotten village

Ayala to survey the enigmatic Gulf of the Farallones. In August, 1775, Ayala anchored within the Golden Gate, proving at least to his satisfaction that the bay chronicled earlier actually existed and could support a colony. The following year Captain Juan Bautista de Anza brought a group of settlers, priests, and soldiers, who established a mission and military garrison as a first step in extending the empire of Spain.

Unfortunately, the colonizing influence of the California missions was negated in 1833 by the Secularization Act, which took away local church powers and caused mission property to fall to government appointed administrators, many of whom were concerned more with swelling their personal holdings than with furthering the influence of Mexico. In a short time Yerba Buena—the tiny village by the big bay—was known only to the few persons who lived there.

Though Mexico had apparently forgotten its northernmost territory, the rest of the world hadn't. England and several other countries were making furtive moves toward California when on July 9, 1846, the American naval Captain, John B. Montgomery, boldly raised the stars and stripes over Yerba Buena.

Under the influence of enterprising Yankees, San Francisco enjoyed a surge of popularity which settled down to slow yet steady growth. Its founding fathers—merchants such as William Richardson, Jacob Leese, Thomas Larkin, W. D. M. Howard, Sam Brannan—were far-sighted men who could sense the potential of the place but who were content to use their native in-

Insurance alley, about 1900—Montgomery Street, between California and Sutter.

San Francisco...a new frenzy

genuity in developing it and their fortunes. San Francisco was on its quiet way to becoming a respectable town when in 1848 fate intervened in the form of gold.

San Francisco became a boom town as well as a ghost town virtually overnight. Though a tide of men poured into the place from all over the world, most stayed no longer than it took to get outfitted and book passage to the diggings. When the gold fever finally died down, San Francisco was forced to find new ways to prop up a sagging economy. Agriculture and world trade seemed one answer, and then as the place was adjusting to a steady, hardworking respectability, fate moved again in the 1860's with the discovery of an unbelievably rich mountain of silver in Nevada.

Though the source of the riches was in another state, the men who knew how to exploit it were not. John Mackay, James Fair, William O'Brien, and James Flood were four perceptive individuals who became fabulously wealthy by controlling the heaviest producing mines in the Comstock, and they started a new frenzy in San Francisco that was all wrapped up in silver, high finance, and railroads.

Completion of the transcontinental railroad brought the city to greater ferment and created a fresh crop of millionaires, among which were Mark Hopkins, Collis Huntington, Leland Stanford, and Charles Crocker.

But millionaires and tumult both tend to fade away, and when the city was once more on its way up from an economic slump, Nature took a hand and the whole place came down in ruins.

1542-1776:

A Frontier Ripe for Conquest

THE AGGRESSIVE CONQUISTADORES had much of the Americas under their control by the middle of the sixteenth century and were casting covetous eyes to the north for new lands to acquire for their king. In 1542 the Viceroy of Mexico commissioned a Portuguese seafarer named Juan Rodriguez Cabrillo to find a northwest passage from the Atlantic to the Pacific and to explore the west coast of North America. Cabrillo landed briefly at the present site of San Diego Bay, then continued north, passing what is now San Francisco Bay. After Cabrillo's death on the return trip south, Bartolome Ferrelo took command and once more drove the ships up the coast, this time going as far as Oregon before being forced back by stormy seas. Although Ferrelo came within seeing range of the Golden Gate four times in all, he was unaware of its existence.

For over two hundred years mariners coursed north and swept south along the California coast, but none seems to have realized that he was passing the entrance to one of the world's greatest natural harbors.

TIMELESS AND UNCHANGING, the rugged coast of upper California in many places looks just as it did some four hundred years ago, when Cabrillo, Cermeno, Vizcaino, and others struck north from Mexico looking for new lands to claim for the Spanish crown.

SPANIARDS, PORTUGUESE, and a most elusive body of water

FREQUENT FOGS, rocky shores, and a ragged, irregular coastline all conspired to conceal the narrow entrance to San Francisco Bay from the eyes of Spanish and Portuguese mariners who sailed up and down California. Though several seagoing explorers passed close to the Farallon Islands between 1500 and 1700—some even stopping there—none seem to have been aware of the break in the shoreline only 30 miles to the east.

IT WAS BY ACCIDENT that San Francisco Bay was discovered. In November of 1769, Gaspar de Portola and his land expedition were looking for the bay of Monterey; overshooting it, they continued north until stopped by a great inland reach of water north of Montara Mountain.

Some Just Sailed on By

For more than 200 years of recorded history, voyagers—seeking a northern strait, new lands, perhaps the legendary "Lost Port" of the Spanish conquistadores—sailed up and down the Alta California coast without discovering the great but hidden inner bay of San Francisco.

Juan Rodriguez Cabrillo set sail from Mexico on June 27, 1542, and explored the Pacific Coast of Baja California. The Portuguese navigator continued up the Alta California coast and reported a "great gulf" (possibly directly opposite the Golden Gate). He was driven back down the coast by severe storms.

Bartolome Ferrelo, Cabrillo's chief pilot, left the Channel Islands February 22, 1543, after Cabrillo's death, and once more worked his way north; he charted the Farallon Islands and twice passed by the bay's entrance.

Francis Drake, English navigator and admiral, landed near latitude 38°, just a few miles above San Francisco, on June 17, 1579. He spent six weeks on the Alta California coast and annexed the land to England under the name "Nova Albion."

Sebastian Rodriguez Cermeno, Spanish army captain, left Manila and reached the Alta California coast on November 4, 1595. Three days later he took possession of the coast and gave the name of San Francisco to what is now Drake's Bay.

Sebastian Vizcaino, Basque explorer and merchant, sailed from Acapulco in May, 1602, passed probably within sight of the big bay, and went as far north as Cape Mendocino.

Not until over 150 years later was the first sighting recorded. During Gaspar de Portola's 1769 land expedition, his chief scout, Jose Francisco de Ortega, reported seeing the southern arm of the bay. Portola himself viewed the bay but was unaware of his discovery.

It wasn't until 1775 that a ship was known to have entered the bay. On August 5, Spanish Navy Lieutenant Juan Manuel de Ayala passed through the Golden Gate aboard the *San Carlos*. His was the first ship into San Francisco Bay.

SAN CARLOS, the supply ship dispatched from Monterey to meet Anza's colonists from Mexico, was two months at sea on her passage up the coast. The ship was the first vessel known to have entered San Francisco Bay.

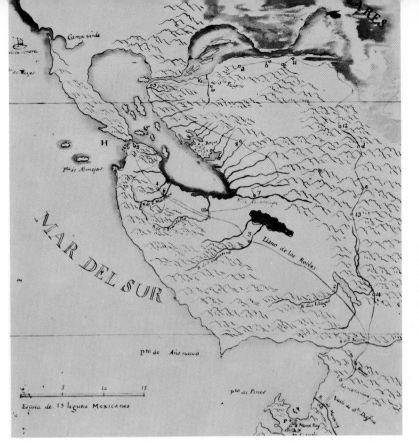

SAN FRANCISCO BAY, as mapped by Father Pedro Font in 1776. Route marked around area was taken by Font, Moraga, and Anza after fulfilling their prime objective of setting up two crosses, one at the location of the future presidio, the other at the place the mission was to be built.

REMARKABLE fortitude was exhibited by Juan Bautista de Anza and his party of settlers, who for three months struggled through the wilderness from Mexico to Monterey. Anza and a small group continued north to establish the sites for the future presidio and mission (see map above).

THE VENERABLE plate of brass – historical fact or comfortable legend?

POINT REYES, named in honor of the "day of the Three Kings," lies 40 miles north of San Francisco. Sir Francis Drake—terror of Spanish shipping in the 1570's—is believed to have repaired his vessel, the Golden Hind, *in the small bay near the top of the picture.*

SIR FRANCIS DRAKE, English gentleman, master mariner, plunderer of Spanish treasure ships that plied the Pacific —yet an enigma to modern scholars, who cannot agree whether he was a sophisticated pirate or a man with a secret mission from his Queen. It was Drake's presence in the western Pacific that alarmed the Spanish into developing California.

REMARKABLE relic, this inscribed plate of brass claiming English possession of California and naming it Nova Albion is believed to have been left by Drake in 1579. Found in Marin County in the 1930's, the plate forms a thrilling display at the Bancroft Library at the University of California in Berkeley.

1776-1825:

The Mission and the Military

AS PART OF THEIR EFFORTS to colonize the New World in the name of the Crown and God, the Spanish set up a series of missions that stretched from the southern half of Baja California to the northern half of Alta California. The purpose of the missions was twofold: to Christianize the heathen Indian, and to act as a nucleus for further colonization by Spain. In conjunction with establishment of a mission, a military garrison was often set up as a show of force to anyone else who might have designs on the land.

San Francisco de Asis was the sixth mission in the California chain, founded in 1776 on a peninsula of land that separated the Pacific Ocean from the port that was reported to be large enough to hold all the ships of Imperial Spain. Not far from the mission, on a strategic promontory where ostensibly it could protect the harbor entrance, was the presidio or fort. In spite of noble aims, both mission and presidio fell into decline, and early in the 1800's they became little more than deteriorating outposts within a neglected settlement.

CIVIL AND MILITARY authority was combined in the delicate office of Gobernador. Don Luis Antonio Arguello was the first appointed Mexican Governor of California, holding office from 1823 to 1825. His grave is surrounded by an iron fence in a shaded corner of Mission Dolores cemetery, adjacent to the original mission building.

THE CHURCH by the lake of sorrows

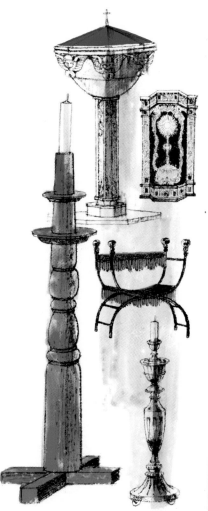

"IF SAINT FRANCIS desires a mission, let him show us his harbor and he shall have one," Inspector-General Galvez told Serra when they were planning Alta California missions. Original name of "St. Francis de Asis" given mission by founder, Father Francisco Palou, was gradually replaced by "Dolores," taken after a nearby lake. In settling the missions, pursuant to establishment of a Spanish colony, one of the first steps was to urge local natives to embrace Christianity. The large wooden candlestick in the drawing of mission details at left was made by local Indians. Below, Indian men dance after Sunday service while priests look on.

CALIFORNIA'S presiding missionary, Father Junipero Serra (opposite page), was insistent on a mission being founded in honor of Saint Francis. Statue of this dedicated man stands in Mission Dolores cemetery.

"SEVERAL HUTS on the waterside...the men go quite naked"

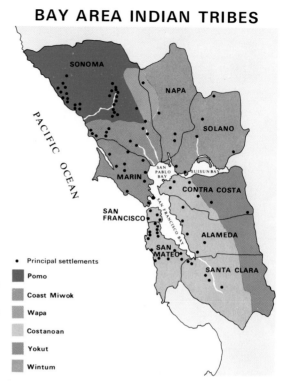

BAY AREA INDIAN TRIBES

SONOMA

NAPA

PACIFIC OCEAN

SOLANO

MARIN

SAN PABLO BAY

SUISUN BAY

CONTRA COSTA

SAN FRANCISCO

SAN FRANCISCO BAY

ALAMEDA

SAN MATEO

SANTA CLARA

- Principal settlements
- Pomo
- Coast Miwok
- Wapa
- Costanoan
- Yokut
- Wintum

TENACIOUS of land rights, the bay region's early Indian tribes kept within sharply delineated territories, their settlements usually strung out along water.

Indians-Earliest Residents of the Bay

Before the white man, the bay region's inhabitants were the California Indians. Enjoying a gentle climate, a sea full of fish, and a year-round harvest—and without the hardships of most American Indians—they languished in a comparatively under-developed Indian culture.

Generally, each tribe lived in small, close-knit tribelets, each speaking a different version of one linguistic family, the Penutian. Their dwellings were dome-shaped structures made from sticks, brush, and reeds. Usually men went naked and women wore loose-hanging skirts of deerskin, tule, or bark fiber; both adorned their faces and breasts with tattoos. Except for the chiefs, monogamy was the general rule. A man would buy his bride with strings of thin shell discs, then live with his wife's people. They speared fish from tule rafts and hunted game with bow and arrow. Acorns were the staple for many, and wild seeds, roots, berries, and greens completed an unusually well-rounded diet. Only the Yokuts made pots; most squaws cooked in watertight baskets and carried their babies in tule cradles.

Before aliens forced their civilization upon the Indians, explorers brought back sympathetic reports. Francis Drake noted in 1579 that the Miwoks handled their bows and arrows "very skillfully" and ran "very swiftly, and long." Father Crespi in 1772 called the Costanoans friendly, and observed that they were "redheaded, bearded, and fair."

WITH THE FOUNDING of the mission, the lot of local Indians improved somewhat, since they were fed, housed, and clothed. This sketch of the presidio (made in 1816 by Louis Choris, a visiting artist) would at first glance seem to indicate a master-slave relationship, but from the free conversation of the group around the fire, the horsemen were probably merely accompanying their Indian charges to the mission or to work in the fields. Native families also had plots of land assigned to them, on which they cultivated melons, fruit trees, and berries.

A MILITARY GARRISON more in name than in fact

CALIFORNIA'S northernmost military garrison was for a long while an outpost in every sense of the word. Established in 1776 (along with Mission Dolores), the presidio was never staffed by more than a handful of Mexican soldiers, and even these few depended on the mission for food. In 1826 the English explorer Captain Frederick Beechey, who entered San Francisco Bay on a mapping expedition, was appalled by the neglect into which the place had fallen. Its fortifications were three rusty cannons that served mainly to prop up a half-dressed sentry. Above, the presidio in slightly better days, in 1806; below, in 1853, after being garrisoned and spruced up by American soldiers.

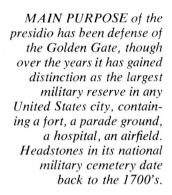

MAIN PURPOSE of the presidio has been defense of the Golden Gate, though over the years it has gained distinction as the largest military reserve in any United States city, containing a fort, a parade ground, a hospital, an airfield. Headstones in its national military cemetery date back to the 1700's.

SPANISH AMERICAN WAR, in 1898, brought troops and transport ships. Alcatraz was occupied by Coast Artillery detachments and was used as a disciplinary barracks.

1825-1848:

Yankees are a Wonderful People

DURING THE EARLY 1800's the shoreside settlement on San Francisco Bay was literally forgotten by the authorities in Mexico City. There was little communication between it and Monterey, capital of Alta California, and practically none with Mexico. The colonists considered themselves chiefly ranchers and between fiestas made the best of their idle time with such diversions as pitting bulls against bears or snatching roosters off the ground while riding by at full gallop.

By the 1830's the place was becoming an international roadstead, a regular port of call for New England whalers, Russian fur hunters, Yankee hide collectors, and English mappers. Sensing that the expanding maritime traffic was but a prelude to greater things, several Eastern-born merchants set up trading posts in town.

With the outbreak of war between Mexico and the United States in the spring of 1846, the Americans moved quickly in California. In June an attempt was made by a band of Yankees to overthrow the Mexicans in Northern California, and they succeeded in establishing the dubious "California Republic" at Sonoma. Early in July Monterey was formally occupied, and almost simultaneously a naval detachment dropped anchor off Yerba Buena. After landing a party of soldiers and marines, the officer in charge ceremoniously raised the Stars and Stripes, thereby proclaiming the village a possession of the United States.

FANCIFUL, ROMANTIC scene of San Francisco in the mid-1800's shows a virtual land of milk and honey. The happy peasants—described as "a group of Mexicans"—could have been lifted straight out of France, which they probably were, since the lithograph was done in Paris.

THE STARS AND STRIPES brought an end to a dozing outpost

AMUSEMENTS for Californians during the early 1800's were lively and characteristic of their exuberant spirit. Picture above shows the popular sport of snatching a buried rooster by the head at full gallop. At right, a bull and a bear are pitted against each other in one of the battles that were "the everlasting topics of conversation with the Californians."

YERBA BUENA, a distant settlement in Alta California, was virtually ignored by the authorities in Mexico City for decades. By the early 1800's the mission (above) was crumbling from neglect, the Indian population had been thinned out drastically by illness introduced by the white man, the presidio was "little better than a heap of rubbish and bones, on which jackals, dogs, and vultures were constantly preying." It was a time of discontent, a time ripe for change.

...END OF AN OUTPOST

THE STARS AND STRIPES *flies over Yerba Buena! In 1835 the United States offered Mexico $500,000 for the northern half of California, to no avail. The world had its eyes on the American west, and England was believed to be negotiating for the province (an Irish priest was even raising funds to bring a group of Catholic colonists over). On July 9, 1846, less than a month after American John C. Fremont's abortive Bear Flag revolt, Commander J. B. Montgomery arrived in the* USS Portsmouth *and raised the American flag.*

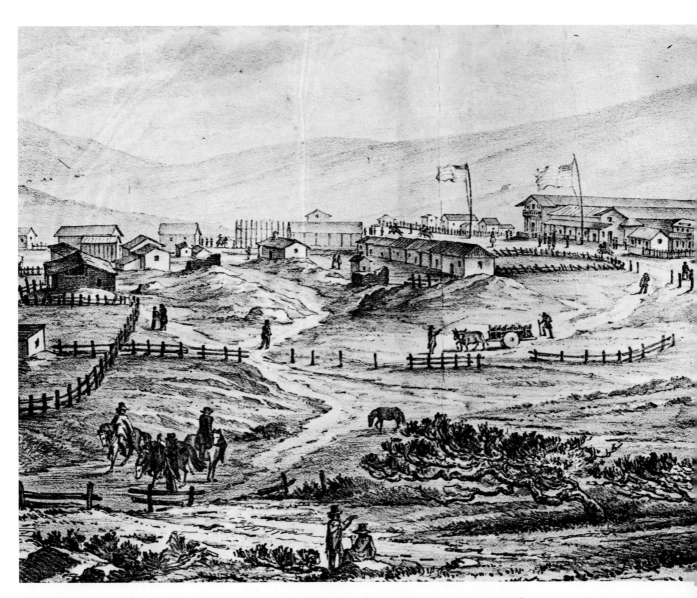

AMERICAN FLAGS wave proudly in a stiff breeze. Shortly after California became part of the United States, newcomers headed into the state from other parts of the country. Most of the residents of Yerba Buena were Americans and Spanish Californians; there were also a few Europeans and New Zealanders. With such a mixed, growing population, activities expanded from the center of town in Portsmouth Plaza out to the mission district.

UNKNOWN ARTISTS of the time depicted San Francisco in mid-1800's. Painting above (which hangs in the fascinating History Room of Wells Fargo Bank) shows the bay lapping at the foot of Telegraph Hill, which is dotted with gold seekers' temporary tents. Picture of Yerba Buena at left was probably made before Gold Rush, judging from the pastoral quality of village and peaceful appearance of the waterfront.

"ONE RESTAURANT...two grog shops ...a blacksmith"

KEARNY AND CLAY, before the middle of the nineteenth century, was already a part of the town's center. The popular City Hotel was originally the store and home of William Leidesdorff, a pioneer business man from the West Indies who became American Vice-Consul under Mexican rule. A French visitor of the time commented that the houses scattered along the shore and on the hill behind the hotel belonged to "foreigners."

...GROWTH OF A VILLAGE

EARLY HAZARDS included mud deep enough to swallow men as well as wagons and pack animals. At one time merchants sank bags of flour, cotton bales, and uncrated cook stoves for a foundation from which they hawked their wares standing. Board walks that were built on the mire became in effect floating bridges.

PORTSMOUTH PLAZA in the mid-1800's bustled with frenzied activity stemming from Gold Rush, and it seemed that the town was here to stay. When mail arrived once a month at the post-office (tall building at far left), lines of waiting men stretched from Clay Street to beyond Sacramento. Building in center is the Justice's Court; on right is the old adobe custom house; in foreground is the horse market. The other sides of the plaza were lined with boisterous gambling halls and amusement houses, where miners who were lucky enough to bring gold dust back from the diggings could part with it with very little effort.

SURE SIGN of growth was the appearance of steamers on the bay. In 1847 William Leidesdorff brought a small boat from Alaska, called—for want of a better name—"The Steamboat." With the discovery of gold, several steamers were shipped in pieces from the Eastern United States and assembled in San Francisco to carry cargo and passengers up the Sacramento and San Joaquin Rivers. Cabin passage to Sacramento was $30, plus $5 if the berth was used.

WHALERS AND TRADERS – the
start of a great maritime trade

YERBA BUENA, original name given to San Francisco, was taken from the mint that grew wild over dunes in the area. The village was a stopping-over place for Russian traders in sea otter fur, who established Fort Ross 90 miles up the coast as a base of operations in California.

ABOVE: Ships waiting to be loaded or unloaded in 1837; probably some of them belonged to the Hudson's Bay Company, which maintained a trading post in Yerba Buena. The artist, John J. Vioget, was the town's first surveyor and a trencherman of renown, once putting away pancakes, stew, steak, tamales, cake, and pie at a single sitting. RIGHT: Transports, a schooner, and a merchantman anchored in Yerba Buena Cove in 1847. Montgomery Street fronts on the water, and the two streets running down to it are Clay and Washington.

1848-1906:

A Time of Wealth
...A Day of Destruction

FOR A COUPLE OF YEARS after San Francisco became a part of the United States, the village dozed on in the California sun. A few more ships came and went, a few more adventuresome souls moved in from the East, but the place remained a remote settlement, relatively untouched by commerce. At the opening of 1848 the population of San Francisco was less than 900.

By 1850, as a result of the discovery of gold in El Dorado County in the Sierra foothills, the place had grown to 56,000, a phenomenal increase of more than 55,000 people in approximately 24 months! Ships from all over the world crowded the harbor, and San Francisco became a marshaling point for one of the greatest mass movements of human beings in history.

After the gold fever cooled and the town settled down to a steady growth, a second boom occurred—the discovery of silver in Nevada. Though in an adjoining state, the bonanza wrought longer-lasting effects on San Francisco than had the discovery of gold.

At the turn of the century the city was fast becoming a sophisticated metropolis. Its adolescence was over—it was a place to be reckoned with. Then in four days, in April, 1906, the heart of San Francisco was destroyed.

SYMBOL OF AFFLUENCE, Nob Hill in the 1870's was crowned with grand mansions that were eloquent reminders to all of San Francisco of new-found wealth. At the juncture of California and Mason Streets stood the solid-as-a-rock home of James Flood; neighbors up the street were Collis Huntington (white house with big windows) and Charles Crocker.

GOLD – the sudden birth and short life of a boom town

THE PLACE WENT CRAZY! This is perhaps the best description of San Francisco in 1848-49 when anyone who could move did so in the direction of the Sierra gold fields, causing the greatest mass migration of human beings in history. Men paced the water's edge, chafing at even an hour's delay in getting transportation. The windjammer Niantic *was one of several ships abandoned by passengers and crew in their rush to the diggings and later drawn up on shore to serve as hotels or stores.*

The Glorious Golden Age of Sail

*Sea Witch, Stag-Hound, Trade Wind, Flying Cloud—names that could send
a shiver of excitement down a man's spine in the mid-1800's.
These were the sleek Yankee clipper ships, built for speed, that
for two decades stormed around the Horn and boomed through the Golden
Gate, making and breaking records with every voyage. Sailing
cards as colorfully romantic as the ships they promoted
encouraged Eastern merchants to send their goods West this way.*

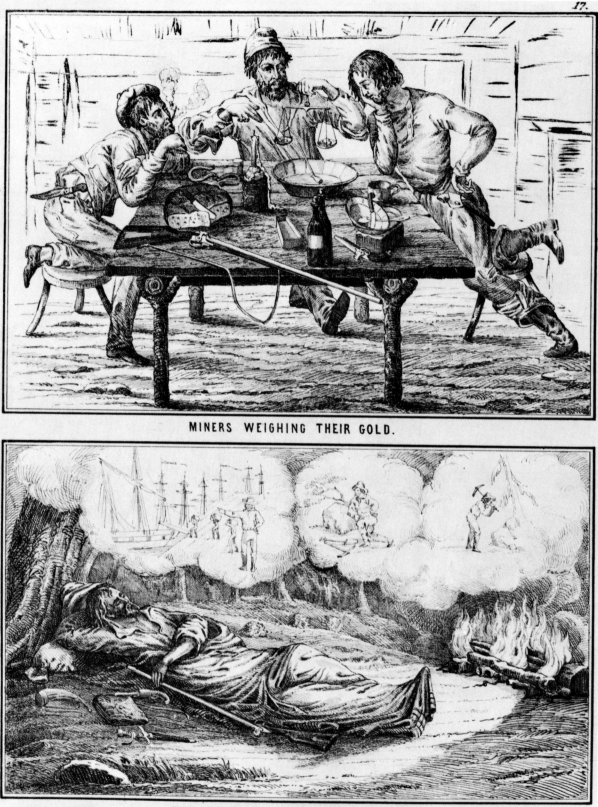

MINERS WEIGHING THEIR GOLD.

THE DREAM OF A PROSPECTING MINER.
Lith. & Published by Britton & Rey corner Montgomery & California St? S. Francisco.

...GOLD, A BOOM TOWN

LIFE AT THE MINES wasn't all it was cracked up to be, and many of the gold seekers who managed to survive came back wiser but richer only in their dreams. One sagacious argonaut—Levi Strauss—never got closer to the gold fields than San Francisco, where he prospered in making tough canvas pants for miners such as the well-attired quartet above.

A SECRET SOCIETY of respectable citizens

FREQUENT FIRES and other criminal depredations by roaming gangs of hoodlums prompted a group of citizens to organize the first Vigilance Committee in 1851 (with ubiquitous Sam Brannan as president), the second five years later. Members of the Executive Committee carried an identifying medal bearing an eye signifying that the vigilantes never slept.

JUSTICE at the end of a rope was the prescribed way of dealing with criminals convicted by the vigilantes. James Stuart, multiple murderer and robber, was strung up on the Market Street Wharf (right), with "an immense multitude present." After the well attended hanging of Joseph Hetherington and Philander Brace in 1856 (above), the vigilantes disbanded, feeling that their point had been made.

NEVADA SILVER brought San Francisco fortunes

HEIGHTS HAD A SPECIAL APPEAL for men who dominated the economic and political life of the state. When they weren't busy downtown enlarging their fortunes, they could gaze out over the city from Nob Hill and at least in thought be master of all they surveyed. Their view to the northeast took in California Street and Yerba Buena Island.

A GREAT PART OF THE WEALTH that came out of Nevada's fabulous Comstock Lode poured into San Francisco during the late 1800's. (The drawing below shows major ore bodies in the Comstock, their dates of discovery, and an indication of the millions of dollars yielded by each.) About the same time, men were growing rich—or richer—from the railroads. The nabobs (wealthy, prominent men) were pleased to have a cable car running up California in the 1870's; it gave them a convenient way to reach the crest of their hill.

Riches from Nevada's Mountain of Silver

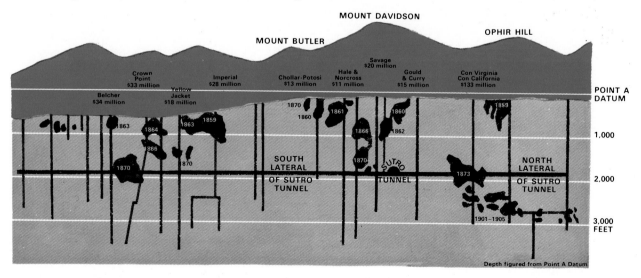

MOUNT DAVIDSON

MOUNT BUTLER

OPHIR HILL

Crown Point $33 million

Imperial $28 million

Chollar-Potosi $13 million

Hale & Norcross $11 million

Savage $20 million

Gould & Curry $15 million

Con Virginia Con California $133 million

Belcher $34 million

Yellow Jacket $18 million

POINT A DATUM

1870

1860

1861

1859

1,000

1863

1864

1863

1859

1860

1866

1862

1866

SOUTH LATERAL OF SUTRO TUNNEL

1870

SUTRO TUNNEL

NORTH LATERAL OF SUTRO TUNNEL

2,000

1870

1873

1901–1905

3,000 FEET

Depth figured from Point A Datum

EL DORADO, a rough and ready gambling house of earlier Gold Rush days, was a raucous place with a bar, an orchestra, and a mixed clientele. The city's second big boom—in silver—saw a more refined approach to relaxation for men (see opposite page). Was it a sign of the times . . . or of more money? Probably both.

The Silver Kings

Bonanza—meaning good weather or, for miners, a rich body of ore—is a Spanish word applied to four Irishmen who realized the American Dream.

Before 1867 John W. Mackay and James G. Fair were miners who had been around San Francisco since Gold Rush days. And James C. Flood and William S. O'Brien were bartenders at the Auction Lunch Saloon on Washington Street, who got into the act as mining stockbrokers.

All four men were savvy to tips on the Exchange. When most people figured the Comstock Lode had hit bottom in the late 1860's, these four started buying into, and later owning, the Hale and Norcross Mine. Then they bought control of the California and Consolidated Virginia. And then they announced in the fall of 1873 their greatest strike, the Big Bonanza of western lore.

San Francisco went mining-stock crazy all over again. The "Nevada Four" syndicate waged a financial war with William Ralston and the Bank of California and went on to tie up the Comstock with their control of milling, water, and lumber. In the end, each of the Bonanza Kings had a fortune exceeding $40 million and a personal history that could thrill a Montgomery Street broker even today.

James G. Fair

John W. Mackay

William O'Brien

James C. Flood

WATERING HOLE strictly for gentlemen of means, Duncan Nicol's Bank Exchange Saloon was a most proper establishment where the loudest sound heard might be the clearing of a dry throat. Situated on Montgomery Street, Nicol's was handy to the financial center of town.

MAKINGS of a millionaire – the railroads

THE RAILROADS ARRIVE! *East of the Mississippi rail lines had existed for several years prior to 1861, but it wasn't until the outbreak of the Civil War that drawn-out arguments over routes linking the East and the West were brought to a head and work went forward on a transcontinental line. The western portion of the road through the Sierra Nevada was constructed by the Central Pacific Railroad Company (now Southern Pacific), the eastern part by Union Pacific. Guiding powers behind Central Pacific were Charles Crocker, Leland Stanford, Collis P. Huntington, and Mark Hopkins—who came into great fortune through its building and subsequent operation. Although the railroad was much more practical than ships for sending goods from coast to coast, it did not immediately create the miracle boom expected in the far West. Since the western terminus of the line was in Sacramento, there was actually a decrease in business in San Francisco, which was at a disadvantage because of its peninsular location.*

END OF PIONEER WEST was marked on May 10, 1869, by the joining of Central Pacific and Union Pacific rails at Promontory Point, Utah. The classic representation of the ceremonial meeting, at which champagne flowed freely and a symbolic spike of California gold was driven, shows decorous officials of both lines, plus a few gate-crashers. The occasion was originally set for May 9 but was delayed until the next day. Never about to let opportunity pass, San Franciscans began their celebration on the 9th anyway and carried the revelry well into the 11th.

CHARLES CROCKER mansion, above, occupied present site of Grace Cathedral. Crocker was foiled in attempt to obtain adjoining property, owned by a Chinese undertaker, and in a fit of pique built a 40-foot high fence around the owner's house. Huntington home (at right) built by David Colton, friend of Crocker, then purchased by Collis Huntington, stood grandly on what is now Huntington Park.

TURRETED *castle at right of picture was built for Mark Hopkins, who employed seven architects. When the Mark Hopkins Hotel was constructed here in 1925, a half-million gallon reservoir was discovered in the courtyard. Site of redwood and marble Stanford home, at left of picture, had a 30-foot stone wall that stretched from California to Pine Street.*

The Railroad Kings

Today, memories of the Railroad Kings are stirred by the names of four big buildings in the city—the Mark Hopkins and Huntington Hotels on Nob Hill, the Stanford Court Apartments nearby, and the Crocker-Citizens Bank.

Mark Hopkins, Collis P. Huntington, Leland Stanford, and Charles Crocker were four men who recognized the value of a dollar. They started their careers as storekeepers in Sacramento and parlayed $50,000 into fortunes estimated at $40 to $50 million each. A desperate nation at war during the 1860's had given these shrewd specu-

lators an empire in return for a railroad—400-foot right of ways, alternate square-mile sections of public land every ten miles of the track, and bonds to finance the track-laying.

With government subsidies and 15,000 Chinese laborers imported especially for the purpose, the "Big Four" built and raced the Central Pacific Railroad eastward across the Sierra and the Nevada desert. On May 10, 1869, they drove the symbolic golden spike at Promontory Point, Utah, linking the westbound Union Pacific to the Central Pacific.

Charles Crocker

Mark Hopkins

Leland Stanford

Collis P. Huntington

WAS IT the quake, or was it the fire?

DISASTER that struck San Francisco on April 18, 1906, was an earthquake-fire, and historians since seem unable to separate the two events. Union Street (opposite page) was but one of several areas heaved and torn apart by violent earth movements. Lower Market Street (above) suffered quake damage but its greatest destruction was by fire that could not be controlled, owing to broken water mains.

...QUAKE OR FIRE?

HOUSES BUILT ON LOOSE FILL were hit hard by the earthquake; they just seemed to sink down and lean in upon themselves. Four square miles of the city were destroyed in 72 hours. Quake or fire? Both: Twelve city blocks between Van Ness and Polk were relatively undamaged but were dynamited to stop the fire.

OVERTURNED stoves and cracked chimneys started scores of fires after the shaking was over. View of California Street on facing page exemplifies tremendous odds that were finally overcome.

Yesterday, today, and tomorrow are all run together in the exciting blend that is San Francisco. This is neither a city of the past nor of the future, but an intriguing mixture of both—which helps explain why it is such an interesting place today.

PORTRAIT OF AN EXUBERANT CITY

Palace of Fine Arts

Ferry Building

Fisherman's Wharf

FROM TIME TO TIME, nationwide surveys are conducted to determine which American cities make the public pulse beat faster. Usually the results are a revelation to the rest of the United States but seldom are they cause for comment in San Francisco, whose boosters have on occasion been accused of not-so-subtle smugness. To them it is only fitting that San Francisco is invariably rated in the top bracket in terms of beautiful setting, beautiful women, good food, lively night life, and uniqueness.

These are the kinds of words that have been written about San Francisco year after year, but they are the kinds of words that—at least to San Franciscans—never grow stale. San Franciscans know that their home has been lavishly written about, praised to the skies, publicized around the world, yet they believe with a passion that it deserves every good phrase devised about it.

Furthermore, San Franciscans take delight even in less-than-kind words about their city. One early writer described the place in the mid-1800's as a perfect hell where common sense had been thrown aside; a few years later someone else stated that quiet and ease were words without meaning in San Francisco. Rudyard Kipling called it a mad city; writer Neil Morgan has termed it an ingratiating failure (and in the next breath, the most enchanting of all American cities). Because such words ring as true as on the day they were written, they are music to the ears of a native because they only confirm his conviction that San Francisco invites damning with faint praise, which makes it all the more a great place. It little matters to him *what* people think

Chinatown's Grant Avenue

Downtown Flower Stall

Japanese Tea Garden

of his city; the fact that they have thought about it has proved the point of the whole thing—San Francisco is a place that captivates.

Much of San Francisco's captivating quality is a result of its refusal to become stereotyped. Rome is known as the eternal city; Paris is the city of light; Los Angeles is a city on the move. Though it has been given dozens of names, San Francisco defies precise definition and logical description.

Located on the tip of a 32-mile-long, hilly peninsula with a land area of slightly less than 47 miles, San Francisco rises from a site where no planner in his right mind would put a city. Where other cities have been able to spread out, San Francisco has had to climb hills. Where other cities have been able to decentralize their activities, San Francisco has had to concentrate its shopping, its housing, its recreation, its industry. As its residents pridefully point out, the city's physical setting has a lot to do with the way San Francisco is; the relative isolation gives them a feeling of independence.

San Francisco is known for its districts that divide the city into smaller, self-contained cities. Some of them define ethnic neighborhoods, others delineate areas of supposed social distinction. Residents are likely to voice strong feelings about their particular district, but few if any can tell precisely where one neighborhood ends and another begins.

The look of yesterday lives in today's homes.

Georgian brick at 2550 Webster.

Curved bay windows at 2038 Union.

Octagonal gazebo at 2645 Gough.

A city of paradox

San Franciscans have seldom been known to be bored, what with a fine selection of sophisticated supper clubs and cabaret-theaters where some of the nation's top entertainers hold forth. The Broadway-Columbus region, with its bright lights and raucous noise, is the center of activity for jazz, foreign entertainment, and highly original nighteries where show girls appear on giant swings or dance atop revolving pianos in performances that hark back to the wildest days of the Barbary Coast. There are three public art museums and scores of art galleries throughout the city. In addition to a glittering opera season, San Francisco has its own symphony orchestra and ballet company; legitimate playhouses presenting the best of Broadway; an annual International Film Festival; and an excellent repertory theater company. Sports enthusiasts can watch the big-league variety of baseball, football, and basketball.

A city definitely on the move, San Francisco moves at its own pace and in its own way. There seems never to have been a time in its history when it deliberately set out with any kind of pre-planned notion of where it wanted to go or how it wanted to get there. Whatever San Francisco has become, it got that way in spite of itself—which is one of the countless paradoxes that charm even its most devoted critics.

Half-arch for non-existent driveway at 1969 California.

Turrets and towers at 2007 Franklin.

Baroque balconies at 2413-17 Franklin.

WHAT MAKES SAN FRANCISCO WHAT IT IS

Hills, Fog... and People

SAN FRANCISCO IS DIFFERENT. Any resident or visitor knows it, and even people who have never been to San Francisco have convinced themselves—with good reason—that it is a very special place, unlike any other city in the world.

San Francisco owes much of its personality to four endowments: its location, its climate, its topography . . . and its people. Surrounded on three sides by water, the city retains the flavor of special remoteness it had in its earliest days. And with an ocean on one side and an enormous bay on the other, San Francisco's weather is tempered to an almost perpetual spring. "The climate is good for the soul," as one native put it, and ". . . it's why we have so many pretty girls."

The skyline of San Francisco is not just another skyline. Downtown buildings poke up in places where they just shouldn't be, according to logic that applies to other cities. But then San Francisco is a place that defies logic.

DIGNITY WITH IRREVERENCE, sophistication with naivety, conservatism with impetuosity. To a marked degree these characteristics describe not only the people of San Francisco, but its physical forms, climate, attitude, and outlook as well. Though the typical San Franciscan is not a stereotype, he would contrast sharply with the casual visitors above.

A CITY ALMOST surrounded by water is bound to be different

"THIS PORT OF SAN FRANCISCO . . . is very large, and . . . could hold not only all the armadas of our Catholic Monarch but also all those of Europe," is how Father Juan Crespi described the magnificent bay some two hundred years ago. The Pacific Ocean has strongly influenced the physical form of the Bay Area, and it continues to bear directly on the activities of the people of San Francisco.

WITHOUT WATER on three sides, San Francisco would perhaps be just another city of buildings, streets, and people. Relative inaccessibility has helped make this a place not only conspicuously different but one with a unique personality.

BODEGA HEAD

TOMALES BAY

Petaluma Creek

SONOMA MOUNTAINS

Napa River

GRIZZLY BAY

Vallejo

SUISUN BAY

SAN PABLO BAY

Benicia

Carquinez Strait

MARTINEZ-BENICIA BRIDGE

Sacramento River

San Joaquin River

DRAKE'S BAY

PT. REYES

Novato

CARQUINEZ BRIDGES

Martinez

Pleasant Hill

Concord

Pinole

San Pablo

San Rafael

RICHMOND-SAN RAFAEL BRIDGE

Richmond

San Pablo Reservoir

Briones Reservoir

BOLINAS BAY

Walnut Creek

Mill Valley

RICHARDSON BAY

Tiburon

ANGEL ISLAND

Berkeley

San Leandro Reservoir

Sausalito

ALCATRAZ

TREASURE ISLAND

OAKLAND

GOLDEN GATE BRIDGE

SAN FRANCISCO-OAKLAND BAY BRIDGE

SAN FRANCISCO

YERBA BUENA ISLAND

Alameda

Livermore

FARALLON ISLANDS

METROPOLITAN OAKLAND INTERNATIONAL AIRPORT

Lake Chabot

P A C I F I C   O C E A N

SAN FRANCISCO BAY

San Leandro

Lake Merced

Castro Valley

DIABLO RANGE

Daly City

South San Francisco

Hayward

Union City

San Francisco International Airport

SAN FRANCISCO INTERNATIONAL AIRPORT

Pacifica

San Andreas Lake

Burlingame

SAN MATEO-HAYWARD BRIDGE

Newark

Fremont

San Mateo

DUMBARTON BRIDGE

Milpitas

Calaveras Reservoir

HALF MOON BAY

Crystal Springs Reservoir

Redwood City

Menlo Park

Palo Alto

Mountain View

SAN JOSE

Woodside

Los Altos

Santa Clara

Los Gatos

SANTA CRUZ MOUNTAINS

N

THE SAN FRANCISCO BAY AREA

Scale In Miles

0   5   10

GEOLOGISTS CONJECTURE *that San Francisco Bay was once a long, rugged coastal depression connected with the Central Valley by a river that flowed out the Golden Gate. One theory says bay was formed when the sea rose as a result of melting glacial ice.*

WEATHER REPORT: Fog in morning, clearing by noon

HEAT—and then the fog. Even the weather refuses to conform to a normal pattern in San Francisco. "Summer" arrives in the autumn, and when October heat bears down and days become uncomfortable, natives watch for the fog to roll in through the Golden Gate.

***THERE ARE** times, though, when nature's air conditioner gets out of control. A thick blanket of fog can lie over the city for days, causing traffic slow-ups and slick streets that provide unexpected thrills for visitors driving down steep hills. Even with sophisticated navigational aids, ships on rare occasion manage to run aground or have a sudden meeting with a bridge pier.*

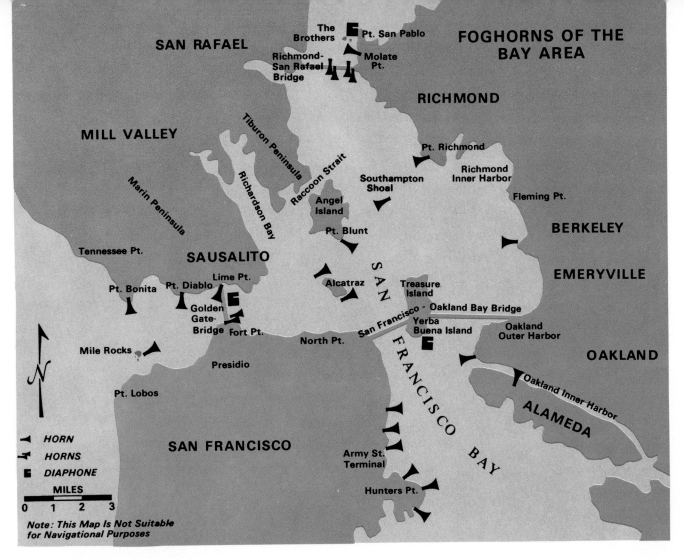

FOGHORNS OF THE BAY AREA

LOCATED at key spots around the bay, foghorns (baritone), diaphones (bellow-and-grunt bass), and sirens (soprano) make up a mixed chorus heard most frequently in July, August, September. By listening closely for a minute or two, old-timers can often tell the position of a fog bank by noting which horns are sounding and which are silent. Chart shows the characteristic signals of principal foghorns in the Bay Area.

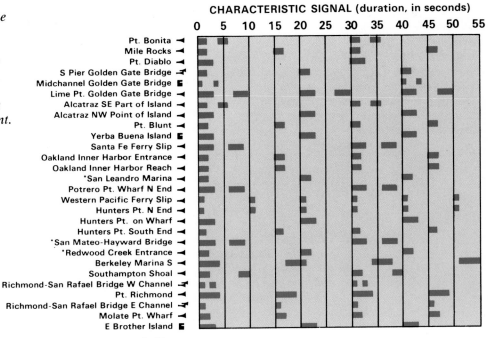

CHARACTERISTIC SIGNAL (duration, in seconds)

Pt. Bonita
Mile Rocks
Pt. Diablo
S Pier Golden Gate Bridge
Midchannel Golden Gate Bridge
Lime Pt. Golden Gate Bridge
Alcatraz SE Part of Island
Alcatraz NW Point of Island
Pt. Blunt
Yerba Buena Island
Santa Fe Ferry Slip
Oakland Inner Harbor Entrance
Oakland Inner Harbor Reach
*San Leandro Marina
Potrero Pt. Wharf N End
Western Pacific Ferry Slip
Hunters Pt. N End
Hunters Pt. on Wharf
Hunters Pt. South End
*San Mateo-Hayward Bridge
*Redwood Creek Entrance
Berkeley Marina S
Southampton Shoal
Richmond-San Rafael Bridge W Channel
Pt. Richmond
Richmond-San Rafael Bridge E Channel
Molate Pt. Wharf
E Brother Island

Not Shown On Map

...THE WEATHER

GOLDEN GATE PARK *may be clothed in mist, while other parts of the city are enjoying sunshine and clear skies. Certain neighborhoods pride themselves as being "banana belts," where warm temperatures prevail in little pockets surrounded by chilly, hazy air. In spite of its reputation as a foggy place, San Francisco is one of the nation's three sunniest cities (after Los Angeles and Denver).*

WHEN THE AIR *is hot and still and the bay is like a lake, you wait it out in your shirtsleeves while the boat rocks back and forth and the sails flap idly.*

NOW THE WIND blows fresh and clean off the sea, driving you past the white city toward inner San Francisco Bay. The air is crystal clear, the sun brilliant. You're running with a great burst of speed, sails ballooning out, water foaming at the stern of your craft. You swing hard around Alcatraz, turn into the wind, and tack again and again, clawing your way back under the bridge and out of the Gate, praying that the wind holds for the rest of the day.

A CITY'S CHARACTER is shaped by the variety of its people

AFTER the initial thrill caused by the city's physical charms has passed, newcomers are struck by the warmth, the open friendliness of San Franciscans. People notice you, people talk with you for no reason other than they like to talk. Natives carry on their daily tasks without becoming so caught up in them they can't pause long enough to be friendly. Whether a blind man or a baby, the individual has a value that is worth more than minutes or dollars.

EXCEPT for the hair they could almost be taken for twins. Evidence of the city's rich racial background is apparent even on the heights of Nob Hill.

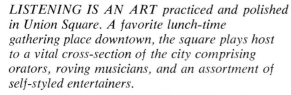

LISTENING IS AN ART practiced and polished in Union Square. A favorite lunch-time gathering place downtown, the square plays host to a vital cross-section of the city comprising orators, roving musicians, and an assortment of self-styled entertainers.

THE CITY'S CHARACTER is best sampled at a busy cable car turnaround. The wide cross-section of people riding, helping to push—or just looking on—includes tourist and resident, bohemian and business man . . . the young and the old. It's a small sampling of a metropolis, but one that illustrates perfectly the rich variety and fascinating contrasts that typify the city.

...THE CITY'S CHARACTER

*MOMENTS OF SECLUSION are respected, no matter what the surroundings. In this city
a man commands respect whether he wants to pursue "Dear Abby" in Union Square,
play a trumpet in Aquatic Park, or, like longshoreman-philosopher Eric Hoffer, read
Shakespeare on the waterfront.*

THE TOPOGRAPHY consists of hills and more hills

THE HILLS may be unkind to mailmen, movers, and parked cars, but a hard-breathing scavenger at work on Leavenworth summed up his feelings in a way that speaks for everyone: "These hills are hell to climb, but ain't it great when you get to the top?" Three streets open to automobiles share title as the city's toughest to climb: Filbert between Leavenworth and Hyde; Arguello between Irving and Parnassus; 22nd between Church and Vicksburg.

WHEN SEEN BY NIGHT from any of its hills, San Francisco has a luminously tiered Oriental appearance. Looking past steep streets at the edge of the Mission District, the eye lights upon the dome of City Hall, the Federal Building, the spire of Grace Cathedral.

83

THERE IS NO ONE SAN FRANCISCO

Cities within a City

MORE THAN ONE RESIDENT of San Francisco has been known to have been born, grown up, and died without ever having left his own neighborhood. While such extreme isolationism is rare, there are today many people who leave their neighborhood only during working hours, and then only long enough to go to work. They would not think of going downtown to shop or for entertainment—all this and more is available just a few blocks from home.

Such fierce regional pride is evidenced by such good-natured admissions as, "I wouldn't live anywhere else but out in the Mission," or "Why go downtown—we've got everything we need right here in the Sunset," or "The weather's better, the view is better, everything is better in the Marina." The interesting fact is that such chauvinism is true. Each district, each neighborhood has something all of its own that makes it a place of substance to its residents.

On a relative scale, the people of San Francisco assign more value to places than to things. And because everyone has his own favorite place in the city, it's why there is no one San Francisco.

*MAIN ARTERY of Little Italy, Columbus Avenue is touched by extensions of Chinatown
and portions of Filipino, Basque, Spanish, and French settlements. Although each culture
maintains its personality, the mixture makes for interesting combinations, such as an
"Italian" market operated by Chinese, a "Chinese" newsstand run by an Italian.*

DOWNTOWN-busy
shopping heart of the city

AT NIGHT THE HEART of San Francisco doesn't just light up—it glows with life. You're looking down from the giddy heights of the Bank of America Building onto Pine Street as it runs eastward toward Market, visible to the right. This is the edge of the city's financial district, a vital part of "downtown" that is filled with hurrying workers by day. At top of photo, the Bay Bridge forms a bright line of lights across the bay.

...DOWNTOWN

LIVELY CENTER of downtown shopping district, Union Square is surrounded by smart shops, fine hotels, and large department stores. Numerous world famed retail establishments offer everything from Paris originals to domestic bird seed.

CITY AND COUNTY OF SAN FRANCISCO

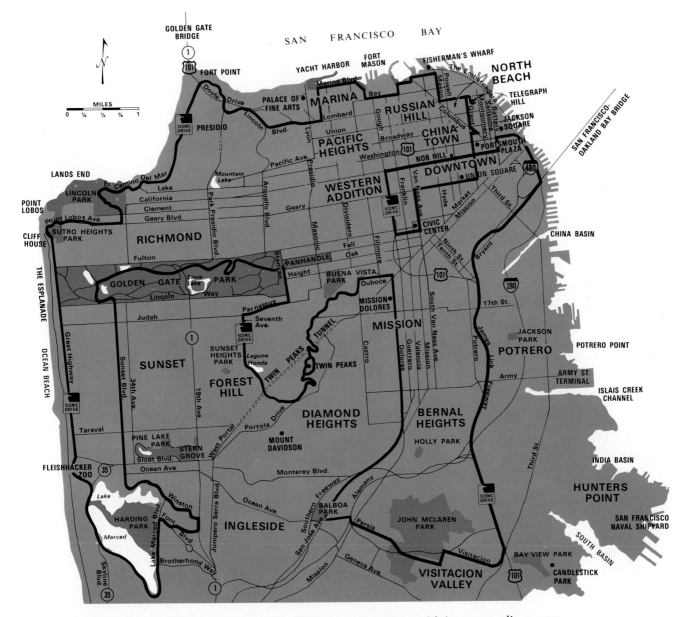

THOUGH RELATIVELY SMALL IN AREA, in comparison with its surroundings—see Bay Area map on page 73—San Francisco occupies a busy, 46½-square-mile peninsula that is the hub of the entire region. From San Jose in the south to San Rafael in the north, and from all over the East Bay, pours a daily flood of humanity that is absorbed chiefly by the city's financial and shopping districts downtown. The downtown area has been called a shopper's mecca in the same sense that London, Paris, and New York are— a world marketplace where anyone can find anything, all within a short walk. Heavy black route on map is 49-mile scenic drive (marked in town by blue and white seagull signs), which covers the city's most important scenic and historic points.

CHINATOWN–principal attraction
for both visitors and natives

PORCELAIN, *cloisonne, jade, and ivory are part of the fun of looking in Chinatown.*
Priceless ball at left is actually more than a dozen spheres that have been
painstakingly carved inside one another from a single piece of ivory. Four-inch
ivory lady is helpmate for modest Chinese women who, in describing ailments to doctor,
prefer to point to afflicted area on doll.

FRIVOLITY AND FINE ART are offered by the shops along and off Chinatown's Grant
Avenue, but you have to look past the gewgaws to find the gems. Open-air stalls
offer everything from thousand-year-old eggs to Wrigley's gum, from authentic
temple gongs to picture postcards of the very shops that sell them.

...CHINATOWN

CHINESE OPERA, held on special occasions, features hours-long performances during which audience drinks tea and socializes to pass the time. Reproductions of classical musical instruments are sold in many Grant Avenue shops.

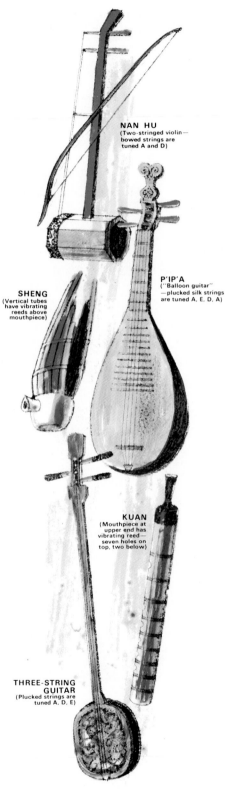

NAN HU
(Two-stringed violin—bowed strings are tuned A and D)

SHENG
(Vertical tubes have vibrating reeds above mouthpiece)

P'IP'A
("Balloon guitar"—plucked silk strings are tuned A, E, D, A)

KUAN
(Mouthpiece at upper end has vibrating reed—seven holes on top, two below)

THREE-STRING GUITAR
(Plucked strings are tuned A, D, E)

POPPING firecrackers and blaring music usher in Chinese New Year, as traditional Golden Dragon is paraded along Grant Avenue during annual celebration that takes place in late February or early March. Visitors escape the crush long enough to admire ivory carvings in a quiet shop.

CITIES WITHIN A CITY **93**

NOB HILL – a history of privilege, a place of prestige

NOB HILL is dignity and decorum that reaches back to the 1800's when it was home for the city's most influential families. It is a place of elegant hotels (above: Fairmont on left, Mark Hopkins on right; at the right, Huntington), urbane apartments, a marble temple (Masonic), a concrete cathedral, and a brownstone men's club that is one of the best known yet most inaccessible places in the entire city.

KNOBBY TREES on Nob Hill cast shadows against fence surrounding the stolid Pacific Union Club, former home of Comstock millionaire James Flood. The stroll along California Street to Grace Cathedral is most pleasant in the summer when the sycamores arch over the sidewalk.

The Big Men on the Big Hill

The Railroad, Bonanza, and Gold Rush nabobs (slang for wealthy, prominent men) gave Nob Hill its name. The first house on "The Hill of Golden Promise," as it was once called, was built by a Dr. Arthur Hayne in 1856. But not until the cable car was running in the 1870's could people easily reach the crest, and it was then that San Francisco's wealthy moved up the hill.

Richard Tobin built the first mansion, which boasted a tower with a spectacular view in all directions. Then the exodus from fashionable Rincon Hill and South Park began, and Nob Hill became *the* address. Leland Stanford, Mark Hopkins, Charles Crocker, and David Colton—Railroad Barons all—built mansions there. Comstock millionaires like James Fair and James Flood lavished their newly found wealth on building sprees, each trying to outdo the other in gingerbread ornamentation and ornate decoration. Objects of art and special building materials came around the Horn in shiploads. Nob Hill was undeniably gay in the Nineties.

Then came the holocaust of 1906. Everything was leveled except the Flood brownstone, now the home of the Pacific Union Club. A marble portico was all that the fire left of a fine home at Taylor and California Streets. Its pillars now stand in Golden Gate Park, appropriately labeled "Portals of the Past."

Many of the wealthy families didn't rebuild on the same spots. They moved away to join artists and writers on Russian Hill or to build garden homes in Pacific Heights —but always with a view. Where most of the mansions stood on Nob Hill, hotels or huge apartment buildings now rise.

NOB HILL offers a delightful
surprise in its pocket-sized
Huntington Park, a refreshing
green oasis sandwiched between
the P.U. Club and Grace
Cathedral where nursemaids
and mothers chat while the
youngsters romp in
the refined atmosphere.

FOUNTAIN of the turtles, in Huntington
Park, was a gift to the city from the
Crocker family. The copy of a Roman
fountain (by Taddea Landini, 1585) has
no turtles, nevertheless it is a pleasant
place to discuss an important affair
of the moment.

GRACE CATHEDRAL'S medieval towers soar
high above California Street. A center
for one of the city's major religious congregations,
the huge structure also houses many fine works of art.

NEIGHBORHOOD solidarity
near the ocean

IT'S NOT JUST THE WEATHER that stimulates local pride in the Richmond, the Sunset, Park-merced, and other communities that share the city's western shore. There are brilliant days when the Farallon Islands stand out against the horizon, and there are days when fog billows past 19th Avenue and rests like drifted snow against the sides of Mount Davidson and Mount Sutro but leaves choice areas in islands of sunshine. And 19th Avenue is a case in point of local pride. After World War II the city proposed turning the thoroughfare into a freeway linking Great Highway with Golden Gate Bridge, as part of a master freeway plan. Residents throughout the area rose as one and carried a fierce battle whose repercussions are still being felt.

HALLMARKS of many neighborhoods west of Twin Peaks are the living room over the garage, bay windows facing the street, a narrow strip of lawn — and a close, comfortable look. The surest way to provoke a resident into a vociferous defense of the district is to ask him if he doesn't feel that the area is a bit cramped.

...NEAR THE OCEAN

FORTUNATE indeed are San Franciscans who live within sight and sound of the water that virtually encircles the city. Residents of areas such as Sea Cliff (at left) or near Bakers Beach (below) are quite used to the waves that pound just inside the Golden Gate. There is geological evidence in this area that some thousands of years ago the level of the sea was fifty to sixty feet higher than it is now. And the ocean continues to wash at the edges of the city; page opposite shows a stretch of Great Highway where it swings past Fleishhacker Pool and in toward Lake Merced in the southwestern corner of town.

Pistols by the Sea—an Affair of Honor

The period from 1850 to 1860 marked a dueling decade in the raucous life of San Francisco. Duels were frequent and sudden during the Gold Rush, reached a pinnacle of popularity in 1854 and 1855, then were on their way out by 1860.

If a gentleman were insulted, he would follow a strict and formal approach to setting up a duel—the challenge, the acceptance, the selection of a site, the appointment of seconds and surgeons, and the gathering of an audience. By all means an audience! Most duels were well publicized and well attended. An early publication states that the lack of an admission charge seemed the only thing that distinguished the entertainment from bull-and-bear fights. Meadows and glades in the outskirts of the city or near the ocean were the preferred locations. Nearby roadhouses featured early morning "Pistols for two and coffee for one."

It was in a valley near the south shore of Lake Merced that the last duel-to-death took place. State Supreme Court Chief Justice David S. Terry had made insulting remarks about U.S. Senator David C. Broderick. When Broderick heard about them and replied with bitter words, notes were exchanged and the duel was set for September 13, 1859. Broderick's first shot missed, Terry sent a bullet through Broderick's chest, and the Senator died four days later.

THE MARINA – boats, carriage houses, and a view of the Golden Gate

PALACE OF FINE ARTS rises like an ornate bubble near western end of Marina District, whose residents enjoy the city's closest inside view of Golden Gate Bridge as well as the rugged hills of Fort Baker Military Reservation in Marin County.

ON WEEK-ENDS *the yacht harbor is a flurry of activity and the bay is a cloud of sails. Host to one of the most popular pleasure craft harbors in the Bay Area (along with Sausalito and Belvedere), the Marina attracts yachtsmen, Sunday strollers, and picnickers to the Green as well as a flood tide of automobiles along Marina Drive and Lombard Street (Highway 101). Much of the area came into being as a result of land reclamation after the Panama-Pacific International Exposition of 1915.*

Sailboat Watcher's Guide

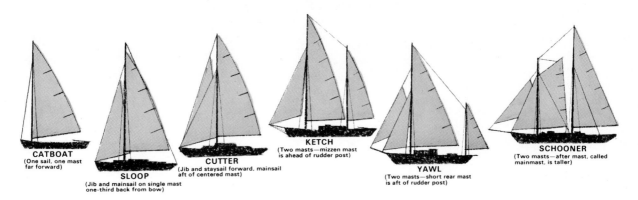

CATBOAT
(One sail, one mast far forward)

SLOOP
(Jib and mainsail on single mast one-third back from bow)

CUTTER
(Jib and staysail forward, mainsail aft of centered mast)

KETCH
(Two masts—mizzen mast is ahead of rudder post)

YAWL
(Two masts—short rear mast is aft of rudder post)

SCHOONER
(Two masts—after mast, called mainmast, is taller)

...THE MARINA

CHRISTMAS season brings traditional chains of lights strung along rigging of boats moored in the harbor. Below, the characteristic architecture of tile roofs and ornate balconies with iron railing is sometimes referred to as Hollywood Mediterranean, and is said to have been inspired during the era of romantic Valentino movies during the thirties.

UNION STREET, opposite, is a walker's street, near the Marina. Once part of the city's dairy center, the street is an intriguing place for exploring flower-filled courtyards that have the nostalgic fragrance of yesterday.

WALL TO WALL living
makes close neighbors

THE HILLS of San Francisco impose some interesting building configurations. Many of the city's fine older homes have breathing space between, even though the sun doesn't reach back too deeply. Entrance is through or past a vertical garden that spills alluvium-like down to the street.

DWELLINGS *that march elbow to elbow across rather than up the hills traverse heights too precipitous for gardens. Such rows are not new to San Francisco, as evidenced in the sketch of Telegraph Hill in the 1870's. When you can't build out and you can't build up, you build close.*

...CLOSE NEIGHBORS

A CITY stacked up on itself (opposite) is the feeling you get when you first see level after level of homes stairstepping up the hills. In the proper light the city looks almost Gothic. In some areas of San Francisco (Sunset, Richmond) wall-to-wall living means a patch of lawn on the streetside and a garden in the rear that encourages back-fence friendships.

THE MISSION – a mixture of racial backgrounds

"SE HABLA ESPANOL" are words frequently seen in store windows in the Mission District, words that reflect the city's earliest Spanish beginnings. Though the Mission is predominantly Latin, and though most of the city's Spanish speaking people live here, they form but part of a blend that includes Negro, Irish, German, and Italian. Above, the Mission Neighborhood Association sponsors a street fair in which everyone participates; below, the wires and the cars and the squeezed-together houses may look like a jumble, but it's home to those who say, "I wouldn't live anywhere else but in the Mission."

A GROUP of almost-triplets with omnipresent bay windows faces on Guerrero Street, a wide, handsomely landscaped thoroughfare that runs through the Mission. Not far away is Mission Dolores, where it all began almost two hundred years ago. The ornate Spanish Revival towers to the right are part of the Basilica, which was built in 1916.

NOT UNCOMMON sights south of Market (an early cable car track gave it the "slot" designation) are a housewife industriously sweeping the sidewalk on Potrero Hill and the sometimes incongruous street names in the Excelsior.

The Short-Lived Montgomery Land Company

In the middle 1860's, astute men of fortune knew that millions were to be made in land as well as in gold and silver. At that time Montgomery Street started at Market and ran north.

South of Market, though, with its Rincon Hill and South Park, was the fashionable heart of the city. So William Ralston, with riches from the Comstock Lode and a 21-year-old millionaire partner, Asbury Harpending, decided to extend Montgomery south to China Basin. They visualized a great tree-lined thoroughfare with parks. The idea was Harpending's, Ralston pledged the backing of his Bank of California, and the two formed the Montgomery Land Company.

The two men eagerly set about acquiring properties. In 1868 they bought key land sections from Market to Howard and put up the 400-room Grand Hotel on the southeast corner of Market.

But, when they attempted to buy property south of Howard to the bay, the landowners, Milton S. Latham and John Parrott of the London and San Francisco Bank, not only refused to sell, but vowed to fight the promoters "every inch of the way." Appeals to the state legislature to condemn the property failed and the Montgomery Land Company was dissolved. Ralston had lost $2,000,000; Harpending's gamble was equally costly. Today, New Montgomery Street extends only two blocks from Market to Howard.

QUIET HILLS and clean streets
south of the slot

A CURIOUS but refreshing place, this region of silent streets removed from the bustle of downtown but overlooking it almost aloofly. When do Potrero Hill's streets come to life? Where are the people who live here? Who tends the flowers fenced off with a piece of string?

LOCAL EVENTS give a neighborhood a sense of identity

ART FESTIVAL at Civic Center (top left) brings participants from all over the city, including a troubadour eager to make his own contribution. Top right: Hulahoopers vie for the neighborhood championship in a Mission Street fair. Below: Fascination, awe, skepticism attend a craft demonstration at Chinatown's Art Festival.

*DOWNTOWN, the annual Maiden Lane spring festival attracts happy crowds
to the city's retail shopping center for music and gaiety that overflows into Union Square
and adjoining streets. Daffodils and other blossoms bedeck store fronts in the Lane,
are tossed from balconies by pretty girls, and are carried home as treasures
by very young ladies.*

IN THIS CITY, you're likely to see anything

AN UNUSUAL CITY, San Francisco is a place that seems to breed unusual sights everywhere. In Golden Gate Park it's liable to be a gentleman dressed to the spats and topper, astride a high-wheeler; over the downtown area it's liable to be the Goodyear blimp skimming the skyline as if seeking a highrise mooring; near the ocean—facing page—it's liable to be a golfer with the bridge looming over his shoulder. (Golden Gate Bridge tower isn't quite as close to Lincoln Park as it would seem; the camera lens has pulled it nearer.)

PAPER FISH flying from a Victorian façade is an unlikely combination anywhere except in San Francisco's Japan Town. Traditionally, Boy's Day is celebrated on May 5 by displaying a paper carp for every male youngster in the family. Whatever the exotic object at the right, it's obviously a bargain.

...YOU'RE LIKELY TO SEE ANYTHING

CARRYING a bike up a hill may seem strange but it means a fast ride down
the other side and a pleasant way of getting around the city. A bright day is matched only
by the sunny disposition of the chair-man, who carries repair jobs to and from
his shop. And even though it's shirtsleeve weather downtown, there must
be snow somewhere.

INDIVIDUALITY IN A CULTURAL MELTING POT

A Pride in Ethnic Distinctions

A SIGNIFICANT CLUE to San Francisco's character is the fact that three out of every ten of the Bay Area's inhabitants either were born outside the United States or have at least one parent of foreign stock. The culture of the city has been enriched by the traditions and folkways of many nationalities, many ethnic groups—Chinese, Japanese, Negro, Italian, Greek, and Russian, to name just a few. Most are blended in with the city's residential mainstream, some live in pockets of their own making. If you want to be in Shanghai, visit some of the back alleys in Chinatown off the main tourist thoroughfare. If you prefer Milan or Rome, go to North Beach where the streets that stretch down from Telegraph Hill intersect Columbus Avenue. Tokyo? A few blocks west of Van Ness is Nihonmachi, an area of tiny, old, side-street shops that offer genuine Japanese art objects, and a stretch of modern buildings that offer the newest look in Japanese merchandising.

CONFORMITY is a term infrequently heard and seldom heeded in San Francisco, which has always prided itself on its individuality and on the singularity of its people. Cultural differences in manner, custom, or dress attract little notice.

LITTLE ITALY-a comfortable tie to the old country

NORTH BEACH: Afternoon sun warming the white fronts of pastry shops and delicatessens and reflecting off the crosses on the many-spired Church of Saints Peter and Paul. The Italians have been an influential part of the city since the 1850's, when a finger of the bay extended between Telegraph and Russian Hills and North Beach was truly a beach.

THE IDEA of bocce ball is to roll a wooden ball toward a smaller ball at the opposite end of a dirt court, until the two just "kiss" (bocce). Though the game is chiefly a reason for afternoon socializing, participants engage in heated but good natured argument. A summer's day might also bring out a varied array of musical instruments for an impromptu concert featuring some unorthodox techniques but favorable results.

CONVERSATION, high spirits, and good food are much in evidence in the Italian community. No delivery man is expected to merely make his rounds; he must have time to discuss Milan's soccer team or to pass judgment on a pretty girl.

...LITTLE ITALY

THE BUTCHER, THE BAKER . . . . Small family operated shops prepare many of the Beach's local specialties. San Francisco's sea air—so it is claimed—imparts a special flavor and texture to the Italian dry salami and crusty bread.

THE LARGEST Oriental community outside Asia

OTHER FACE of Chinatown is not always apparent to the casual visitor. Cultural identity is preserved in Nam Kue School with instruction in calligraphy, Chinese language, history, and literature. At far right, a helpful kibitzer contributes to Chinese chess game in Portsmouth Plaza ; below, herbalists compound an exotic prescription.

ONE OF MANY formal groups dedicated to helping immigrants cope with unfamiliar surroundings, On Ping Association derives its name from a district in China. Created originally for protection against early prejudice and exploitation, such organizations today have great value in maintaining business and social contacts in the community.

WINTER RAINS MAY MUTE bright colors of Chinatown's streets, but they also help bring out umbrellas in a profusion of pastel shades, as local housewives make their rounds of markets, checking the quality of fresh produce in sidewalk displays.

...ORIENTAL COMMUNITY

TWO CHINESE DELICACIES of high esteem are dried fish—brought to juicy tenderness by steaming—and golden, roast duck, which hangs glistening and dripping in shop windows until cut up for the table. The sight of both is as much a part of the Oriental community as is the blend of exotic smells and sounds in Chinatown's side streets and back alleys.

JAPAN TOWN – new look in the Western Addition

NIHONMACHI means Japan
Town, but it means more than just
a multi-block area off Geary,
bounded by Laguna and Fillmore.
One of the exciting projects of
the city's Redevelopment Agency,
Nihonmachi furthers Japanese
customs and trade in a complex of
modern shops and showrooms.
Detail at right is from the luxurious
Miyako Hotel, which features
Japanese-style sunken baths.

PEACE PAGODA and Plaza are central features in this bit of modern Japan. There are several restaurants serving Japanese foods; showrooms displaying stereo components, television, and automobiles; and shops where you can watch potters at work or classes in classical flower arranging. The spring Cherry Blossom Festival has become an annual event in Japan Town.

YOU CAN TRAVEL the world without leaving the city

EARLY SOME MORNING, go to one of Chinatown's back alleys, or roam the side streets off Columbus Avenue. Half-close your eyes, sniff the air, and let the sounds flow in and out of your ears, and you'll be in Hong Kong, or Naples.

Headlines of a Rich Racial Potpourri

Your background is Hungarian—or Danish or French or Irish or German or Russian. You want to keep in touch with your heritage but don't feel like an evening at a Japanese theater or a Greek taverna or a Mexican cantina. So you read in any of a score of the city's newspapers about floods in Dublin or credit cards in Zurich or crops in Normandie or medical centers in Stockholm. In San Francisco you may be a newcomer but you're never a foreigner.

...TRAVEL THE WORLD

VENERABLE veterans of old New York and London, two open-top double-deck busses make their daily rounds on a leisurely loop trip of the North Waterfront, starting from Ghirardelli Square, while kids and grown-ups alike whoop it up.

SPUTTERING motor driven rickshaw bumps and jostles its passengers on a fun ride through Chinatown. Handy for squeezing through crowded streets, the small vehicle is reminiscent of Hong Kong or Macao.

San Francisco's Mixed Background

San Francisco has an international birthright. Six flags (of England, Spain, Mexico, Russia, the Republic of California, and the United States)—flew over the region between 1579 and 1850. The frenzy for gold drew people of all nationalities to the port city. The result was a multiplicity of tongues that often caused unusual misunderstandings.

A trial in nearby San Jose in the 1850's was typical of some of the ways San Francisco had to adjust to its melting pot. A Tartar had been accused of assault by a Spaniard. But proceedings were delayed because the Tartar and his witnesses could not speak English. At last a Tartar named Arghat was discovered who could speak Chinese, and a Chinese named Alab who could speak Spanish. So the trial proceeded in four languages.

With many such adjustments San Francisco has become a city that encourages its immigrants to preserve their cultural identities. The 1960 census ranked Italy first as a source of foreign stock in the city, then Germany and Ireland (followed by the United Kingdom, Canada, Mexico, Russia, Sweden, France, Poland, Austria, and Portugal). However, not long after the 1965 Federal Immigration Law Revision removing restrictions on the entry of Asians to the United States, the city's Chinese population grew to more than 55,000, and the Japanese to more than 11,500. Three distinct cultural communities lie within the city: Chinatown, the largest settlement of its kind outside Asia; North Beach, a "Little Italy" to San Franciscans of Italian extraction; and Nihonmachi, Japan Town, a concentration of Japanese businesses and the site of the $15 million Japanese Cultural and Trade Center.

HOW TO LIVE ON THE TIP OF A PENINSULA

Places People Call Home

SOME SAN FRANCISCANS live in big houses, some in small houses; some live in new houses, some in old houses (others—a good many of them—prefer apartment living). Since the city is a city of hills, many of the dwellings most characteristic of the place sit cozily close to their neighbors. In a city where horizontal space is at a premium, this "wall-to-wall living" may seem crowded but it makes good sense.

Some interesting contrasts are to be found in the places people call home. In areas such as Presidio Terrace or St. Francis Wood, handsome residences sit far back from the street, with lawn areas and gardens surrounding them and separating one from the other. In Presidio Heights or Pacific Heights, many of the structures stand close together but extend in a vertical direction for two or more stories—"one-family homes with two-Cadillac garages," they've been called. In districts such as the Sunset and the Richmond, homes march on for miles, elbow to elbow, back garden to back garden.

Residents of the city's bedroom communities may live fifteen to fifty miles out of the town, nevertheless many of them proudly give their home town as San Francisco.

ROW ON ROW they step up the hillsides, flat fronts and peaked roofs catching the afternoon sun. Land is precious in a city virtually surrounded by water, and houses nestle closely. There is an "at-home" feeling about the bay windows oriented to the last light and the clothes lines stretched over the back yard.

AN EXUBERANT CITY   **137**

SOME HOUSES
are bigger than others

GRAND MIXTURES of Tudor, Colonial, Renaissance Revival, and San Francisco Riviera characterize splendid areas where the city's social, business, and political leaders reside. The mansions cluster in several distinctive districts—Pacific Heights (whose quiet neighborhood is shown at left), Presidio Heights (opposite page), Sea Cliff, St. Francis Wood, Forest Hill.

"ALONG THE WALL" refers to the western edge of Presidio Heights where it overlooks the fine wooded acres of the presidio. Many of the three-story, one-family houses are shingled and weathered to a deep brown, giving the neighborhood a feeling of substance, a feeling that is certainly not diminished by the front of a Rolls Royce peeking over the wall.

PLACES PEOPLE CALL HOME   **139**

A Window on the World

You can learn a great deal about a city and its residents by observing its windows. Like the people behind them, windows can be carefree . . . or dignified . . . or fussy . . . or spartan . . . or quiet . . . or bold. Size isn't important; personality is. A window, or a city, usually is not special because it's big—it's special because it has a personality all its own.

...BIG HOUSES

DISTINGUISHING FEATURE of many of the city's distinguished homes is a grand gate. Somehow, a gate is mutely eloquent about the grandeur of the residence that lies beyond.

SURPRISES in a busy metropolis – pockets of urban seclusion

TUCKED AWAY from the casual observer are a wealth of tiny rural spots that would be out of place in any other modern city but seem right in character in San Francisco. The back side of Telegraph Hill is a delightful maze of wooden walks and steep steps overgrown with fern and ivy that—along with the aged houses— make the area look much as it did a couple of generations ago.

HIDDEN FROM THE EYE of everyone except local residents of Russian Hill are tiny lanes where the sun filters through branches or a picket fence to warm a carpet of fallen leaves. Such places are known only to the people who live nearby or to the curious stroller bold enough to push open a sagging gate.

EASTERN SIDE of Telegraph Hill is a mass of jagged rock, painfully bare in many places, but home for cliff hangers. In the early 1900's rock was quarried by casual blasting, so much to the disregard of residents that several houses were brought down or severely damaged until the practice was stopped. San Franciscans like their greenery, whether it covers the house, is confined snugly behind a wall . . . or is cultivated in small containers.

SHARING the view in a city of hills

TIME WAS in San Francisco when hills
were hills and almost everyone who lived on one
could enjoy his favorite view. Now,
with the growth of the city upward, it's not
enough to reside on a hill—you often have to
live in one of the tall buildings in order to see
over another tall building on the next hill.
The drawing below shows comparative heights of
several hills as they would appear squeezed
up close to one another, disregarding relative position.

Do You Look at-or Over-a Hill?

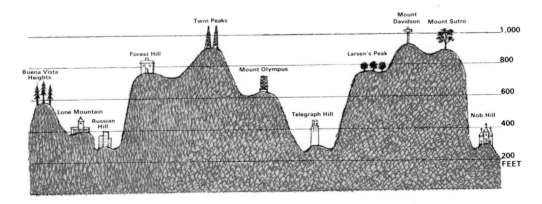

THE PART-TIME San Franciscans –
Where do they come from?

BEDROOM COMMUNITIES of the city are in large part down the peninsula from Burlingame to Palo Alto, though some rail commuters live as far south as San Jose. The grim visage is a result of the end-of-line interruption to the daily bridge game, or else is caused by anticipation of the walk downtown from the Third and Townsend depot.

EVENING TRAFFIC streams over Golden Gate Bridge, carrying Marin residents home or bringing San Franciscans back after a Sunday out of the city. The only link between San Francisco and the north, the bridge experiences traffic jam-ups during peak periods that have prompted studies on how to increase vehicular capacity on the bridge and its approaches.

EBB AND FLOW of the human tide extends south of the city to the constantly expanding International Airport. A great amount of world traffic moves by air in and out of San Francisco, but perhaps as important to the commerce of the area is the efficient commuter service between the city and Los Angeles.

...PART-TIME
SAN FRANCISCANS

GRAND ISOLATION on the unspoiled slopes of Mount Tamalpais in Marin is what some commuters look forward to after a workday in the city. "Tam's" sleeping Indian maiden profile is a familiar sight to the north from San Francisco.

WATER-SIDE communities around the Bay Area are quiet during the work week but come alive with small boats on Saturday and Sunday. Marina living is becoming increasingly popular along the shores from Oakland to Redwood City, from Alameda to Belvedere.

SHADED PATIOS mark long-established residences in Palo Alto, Woodside, San Mateo, Burlingame, Hillsborough, Atherton, and other garden spots down the peninsula. Much of the daily population of San Francisco leads two lives—a working life in the city and a home life out of the city.

A Home Away from Home

The 1860's marked the beginning of the peninsula commute, when building mansions south from San Francisco became fashionable among the wealthy. One of the earliest peninsula commuters, banker William Ralston, made the trip to his suburban estate with his own version of a pony express. The San Francisco and San Jose Railroad line had just been finished in 1864, and Ralston took pride and pleasure in daily races with the train. He frequently won—careening his buggy along the dusty Mission Road at breakneck speed, stopping only at key points for a fresh team of horses.

Ralston built "Belmont," a four-story, eighty-room edifice with banquet hall, ballroom, cut glass doors, silver door knobs and panels, parquet floors, and mahogany-panelled stables. When he died in 1875, his partner William Sharon took over the lavish estate, which is now part of the College of Notre Dame in Belmont.

Financier Darius Ogden Mills selected his homesite in the Buri Buri Rancho, which covered a section of present-day Millbrae and Burlingame. His three-story "Millbrae" had mother-of-pearl and ebony in the master bedrooms and a huge porch overlooking the bay. Apartment houses now stand on the site of Mills' estate.

Probably the most famous peninsula estate known today was Leland Stanford's farm in Palo Alto. It was on his horse farm that Edward Muybridge, father of the motion picture, conducted his photographic experiments. Stanford donated much of his peninsula property to create Stanford University as a memorial to his son.

Nearby in Menlo Park, James C. Flood, of Comstock fame, built what some labeled Flood's wedding cake. "Linden Towers," which stood in what is today called Lindenwood, had three stories topped by a three-story tower, other lesser towers, and elaborate chimneys.

Another banker, John Parrott, selected the Baywood area of San Mateo for a Victorian home, and a retired miner, Alvinza Hayward, built "Hayward Park" nearby, which included a deer and elk preserve as well as a race track. Neither home stands today.

Turning the Wheels of Commerce

AN IMPRESSIVE PORTION of world finance is controlled from within the skyscrapers of San Francisco's financial district, and the city is home of four of the nation's fifty largest commercial banks, including the world's largest, The Bank of America. San Francisco is headquarters of the 12th Federal Reserve District; and the Pacific Coast Stock Exchange holds a prominent place among the country's largest regional security markets. Represented in San Francisco are more than 675 insurance carriers, agents, and brokers.

Traditionally the leading world trade center of the Western United States, and the nation's "Gateway to the Pacific," San Francisco has responded to the needs of the world by making available matchless facilities and a rich fund of economic experience. One of the world's great seaport cities, San Francisco serves a large number of shipping lines which contact at least 300 of the world's ports.

Of all manufacturing, food processing is the largest in volume of product turned out, with printing second. Apparel, fabricated metals, machinery, and chemical products are produced in impressive quantity.

FINANCIAL DISTRICT'S CROSSROADS, *California and Montgomery Streets are a beehive of business activity. California is variously known as Insurance Alley and Shippers' Row; Montgomery is called Wall Street of the West and the Street of Banks.*

BANKS and brokerage houses – financial strength for the Pacific Coast

ANXIETY and relief, concern and pleasure, mark faces of the men watching the big chalk board at the Pacific Coast Stock Exchange. The Exchange is unique among the nation's securities markets, having one trading floor in San Francisco and another in Los Angeles, 400 miles away, connected by direct voice communication. The time differential between the Atlantic and Pacific seaboards makes this the nation's leading securities market after 12:30 P.M. Pacific Standard Time each market day.

ELOQUENT COMBINATION of massive columns and equally massive automobile on California Street speaks of the stability of the city's financial center. Adjoining Montgomery Street is flanked with banks and brokerage houses, which contribute to the nickname "Wall Street of the West."

The Big Bankers

The golden era of San Francisco banking was actually a silver era. During the Gold Rush—1848 to 1850—almost any storekeeper who had scales and a safe to weigh and store gold dust, was a "banker."

But in 1859, when Nevada's Comstock Lode started to flood California with its silver riches, San Francisco became the financial capital of the West. In 1864, speculators Darius Ogden Mills and William C. Ralston organized the Bank of California and successfully plunged into high-risk mining ventures. William Sharon, "King of the Comstock," cashed in on Comstock madness, the gambling surge for mining shares when stock certificates were hawked on street corners.

Ralston was financing everything from Hunters Point drydocks to South of Market real estate to such edifices as the Grand and Palace Hotels. After the bank failed in 1874, and Ralston swam to his death off North Beach, Sharon and Mills decided to refinance, reorganize, and reopen.

The earthquake and fire of 1906 started the rise of another banking giant, A. P. Giannini. Using his stepfather's vegetable wagon, he rescued and camouflaged the gold resources of his fledgling bank and carted them through the ruins to the safety of his home on the peninsula. Thus his bank, the Bank of Italy (now the Bank of America) was one of the first to honor withdrawals after the conflagration.

William Sharon

Darius Ogden Mills

William C. Ralston

A. P. Giannini

PORT OF CALL for world-oriented shipping

THIS PACIFIC PORT has known days during the Gold Rush when there were so many ships jammed in the bay it was easier to abandon them than to move them, days during World War II that ships headed for the Pacific had to be loaded at anchor because there were not enough docks to accommodate all of them.

155

...SHIPS AND SHIPPING

HOME BASE for many of the world's steamship lines and agencies, the Port of San Francisco shares honors with the Port of Oakland as a Pacific Coast leader in general cargo volume, freight, and passenger sailings. Ships in and out of the bay carry newsprint, coffee, copra (dried coconut), grain, cotton . . . and passengers. A favorite pastime of maritime buffs is watching the stately cruise ships sail under the Golden Gate Bridge.

Ships and Service—Two-Way Traffic to Everywhere

On the day in 1775 that the Spanish supply ship San Carlos slipped through
a tide-torn channel to drop anchor in a mysterious, seemingly limitless
harbor, history had a new port of call. Since then, the Bay of San Francisco
has been a constant witness to the coming and going of ships of all sizes,
all nationalities, and the Embarcadero has been a showplace for flags and
insignias of steamship lines that serve the entire world.

CIVIC CENTER–seat of city and county government

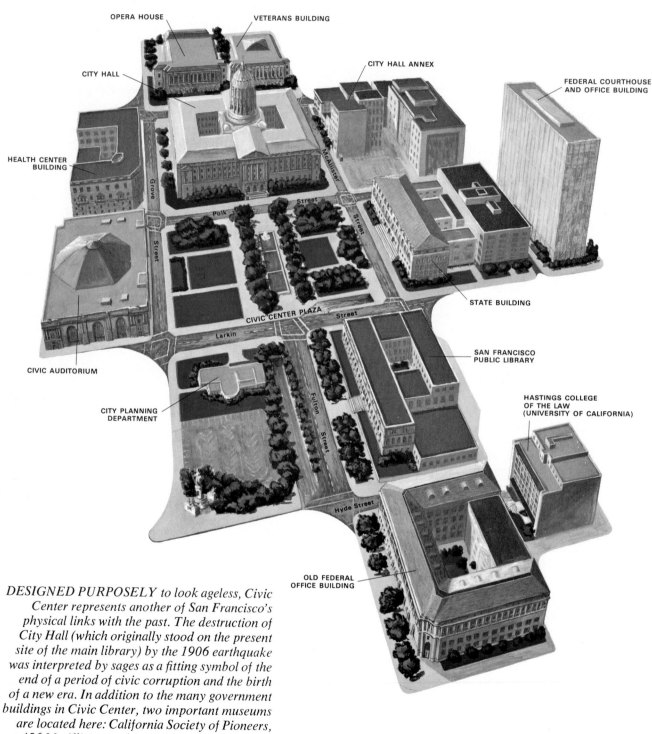

OPERA HOUSE

VETERANS BUILDING

CITY HALL

CITY HALL ANNEX

FEDERAL COURTHOUSE
AND OFFICE BUILDING

HEALTH CENTER
BUILDING

McAllister

Grove

Street

Polk

Street

Street

STATE BUILDING

CIVIC CENTER PLAZA

Street

Larkin

SAN FRANCISCO
PUBLIC LIBRARY

CIVIC AUDITORIUM

Fulton

Street

HASTINGS COLLEGE
OF THE LAW
(UNIVERSITY OF CALIFORNIA)

CITY PLANNING
DEPARTMENT

Hyde Street

OLD FEDERAL
OFFICE BUILDING

DESIGNED PURPOSELY to look ageless, Civic Center represents another of San Francisco's physical links with the past. The destruction of City Hall (which originally stood on the present site of the main library) by the 1906 earthquake was interpreted by sages as a fitting symbol of the end of a period of civic corruption and the birth of a new era. In addition to the many government buildings in Civic Center, two important museums are located here: California Society of Pioneers, at 456 McAllister; and San Francisco Museum of Art, on the top floor of the Veterans Building.

158   AN EXUBERANT CITY

CITY HALL is home to the city's board of supervisors, a name normally given to county lawmakers, but applicable to San Francisco's executive body because the city and county are synonymous. The Renaissance architecture is commonly referred to as "classically extravagant," a description that would have delighted James Rolph, Jr., mayor during the period the hall was built. View at right is from Opera House, where in 1945 the United Nations was founded.

CONFIDENTIAL discussion is held on one of the galleries overlooking the vast rotunda in City Hall, a showplace that has seen demonstrations, state funerals, banquets, and a grand celebration of the 63rd anniversary of the 1906 earthquake.

LATEEN-RIGGED BOATS of the original Sicilian fishermen are no longer seen along Fisherman's Wharf, and the high-sterned Chinese junks are long-gone, but gulls still scream over the day's catch of crab and fish when the pastel-colored, gasoline powered boats chug their way through the Gate back to the wharf in mid-afternoon. The commercial crab season opens early in November and ends around the middle of June or July. On facing page, stoical fishermen coil their lines under a very watchful eye.

COLLECTING the sea's bounty at the city's doorstep

"YOU WANT IT CRACKED?" This is Fisherman's Wharf: A mixture of exciting noises,
blazing colors, brilliant lights, unusual flavors, enticing smells.
The sound of the crab vendors crying their wares along restaurant row; the
sight of steam billowing out of cauldrons; the flavor of fresh shrimp; the smell
of the sea. No matter how long you've been a part of the city, you can
feel the excitement that is the Wharf every time you go there.

ALIVE AND KICKING, crabs go straight from the water to retail outlets. Commercial traps (see drawing) are planted on bottom along the surf line, baited with bits of fish. Crabs enter the cages easily but can't get out a wire trapdoor that closes the opening.

How Crabs are Caught

HERE, the farmers still come to town

LITTLE KNOWN except to old-timers and bargain hunters, the city's Farmers' Market is an open-air complex of stalls and walkways where fresh produce from all over the state is available at low prices.

STRAIGHT FROM THE FIELD, melons are unloaded from truck to booth. The retail Farmers' Market, at 100 Alemany Boulevard, just west of the Southern Freeway, should not be confused with the city's wholesale produce district on the east side of the freeway.

FREE SAMPLES and quantity prices. An Old World atmosphere prevails, since most of the growers are Oriental, Portuguese, or Italian, and some good-natured haggling is in order. Many items are available here that are not always readily found in supermarkets, such as savoy cabbage, long Chinese beans, leeks. Apples, obviously, appear in great variety and quantity.

ALL PART OF THE GOOD LIFE

A Special Respect for Culture

THE LUSTY GOLD RUSH ERA was in large part responsible for the development of a cultural background for San Francisco. Though most of the men who streamed into the city by the Golden Gate returned from the diggings poorer than before, each brought a share of his own background or some special talent to a place that was game to try anything. Diversions of the time included multi-lingual musicians, clamorous music halls, and all-male promenade concerts.

As the city grew, women became less a rarity, men who had come into wealth became gentlemen, their ladies became ladies, and discriminating citizens determined that the rough-shod entertainment should at least be tempered with refinement. Several private gambling houses were formed, some saloons became more selective in their clientele, and a process of social selection began.

By the time of the Silver Rush, leading families decided that the good life wasn't just going to happen, and what San Francisco didn't have it wasn't going to sit and wait for. It was a matter of pride that San Francisco should not lag behind in such matters, so with the opening of the transcontinental railroad eastern artists and entertainers were imported in large numbers.

PROPERLY AWED young lady is distracted at a moment that seems to at least visually sum up the city's attitude toward culture. As one writer has said, San Francisco's relationship with the arts has often been stormy . . . there have been quarrels, recriminations, and separations—but there has rarely been indifference.

THE BIG THREE of the art world

FRENCH NOTE is struck at the California Palace of the Legion of Honor, grandly overlooking Lincoln Park and the Golden Gate. A rich repository of Rodin bronzes (The Thinker sits in the courtyard), the Legion contains French antiques and paintings, many paintings of other schools, and the largest collection of drawings and prints in the West.

FIRST CONTEMPORARY art museum in the West, San Francisco Museum of Art is home to magnificent works by Matisse, Picasso, Braque, Utrillo, and others. Always in step with the times, the museum in the War Memorial Veterans Building in Civic Center hosts exciting displays of sculpture on a grand scale, experimental photography exhibits, and even classic comedy film showings.

CITY'S OLDEST MUSEUM, the M. H. de Young Museum sits in the midst of pines and eucalyptus in Golden Gate Park, adjoining the lovely Japanese Tea Garden. A repository of European and American art, the de Young houses the famed Brundage Collection of jades, Chinese bronzes and ceramics, and Khmer sculpture.

...THE ART WORLD

*NOT ALL of the city's art is committed to life under a museum roof. The vital work of Benny
Bufano, San Francisco's beloved sculptor-in-residence, graces playgrounds, parks,
parking lots, and plazas where children can clamber on it and adults
can experience its forms under the open sky. Benny's studio, a one-time warehouse in
a downtown alley, is crowded with delightful stone animals and many
interpretations of the peace-inspiring patron saint of the city, Saint Francis.*

JUNK SCULPTURE rises humorously yet with earnest intent on mudflats along the east shore and in the south bay. Startling to passing motorists at first, it has now become almost a landmark. San Francisco Art Institute (below), a bubbling center of painting, sculpture, photography, ceramics, and printmaking, is a nucleus of living art and stimulating experimentation.

THE GRAND HOTELS-gold service for visiting royalty

WHERE HORSES ONCE CLATTERED, you now enjoy lunch in an elegant setting. Before the earthquake and fire of 1906, the Garden Court of the Palace Hotel (now Sheraton-Palace) was a palatial carriage courtyard. Today it is a fashionable meeting place for breakfast, lunch, and buffet dinner. Under its high, stained-glass dome have dined presidents, princes, and kings.

...THE GRAND HOTELS

LONG A FOCUS of social pageantry, the St. Francis is a favorite with business people because of its central downtown location. The original St. Francis, built in 1849 at the corner of Dupont (now Grant) and Clay, was termed the fashionable house of the day where the elite of the city boarded or congregated, a description that is as appropriate today as it was then.

"THE MARK" retains the carriage entrance of the old Nob Hill mansion of its namesake, Mark Hopkins. A prime stopping place for visitors, the famous "Top of the Mark" gives a breathless view of the city that is only slightly marred by nearby high-reaching structures.

174 AN EXUBERANT CITY

ORNATE CLOCK is old-time trademark of Nob Hill's other splendid hotel. The Fairmont is a grand collection of established restaurants and lounges, though some upstarts identify the hotel's "new" outside elevator overlooking Powell Street as "the thermometer."

WORLDWIDE RESERVATION service is provided at San Francisco Hilton, a modern and popular hostelry with an open-air swimming pool on its 16th floor. Other of the city's first-rate hotels include the Clift, whose Redwood Room is an institution among theater goers, and the Handlery Motor Inn, which sits on the site of the old Alcazar Theater.

A RICH VARIETY in the performing arts

SAN FRANCISCO'S history of the theater reaches back to Gold Rush days, when dance halls and saloons featured accordionists and fiddlers to add to the overall merriment. Leading citizens of the time were quick to create a pattern that would polish the rough edges of music hall entertainment and establish a social cohesion to the city's culture, a pattern that has prevailed to this day. At left, a dramatic moment from "Ernani," with Leontyne Price and Renato Cioni; above, a different mood prevails during an agitated scene from "Barber of Seville."

ONE OF LEADING dance groups in
the West, San Francisco Ballet enriches
the cultural scene of the city with a
classical and contemporary repertoire.
Though the company has a worldwide
itinerary, its open-air performance in
Stern Grove is favorite to many devotees.
Knowledgeable San Franciscans arrive
hours early to watch the rehearsal,
equipped with hot coffee to ward off the
chill of possible morning fogs.

CLATTERING CASTANETS, clapping hands,
and fiery guitar music provide rhythm for the
exciting dances of a flamenco group. The Spanish
heritage of the city probably has been instrumental
in an unabated interest in flamenco long after it
faded in popularity in other parts of the country.
In addition to performers in clubs, there are
several Spanish dance companies in the city.

EBULLIENT ARTHUR FIEDLER has been conducting members of the San Francisco Symphony in the spirited Pops Concerts since 1950. The mid-summer programs feature promising young artists, many of whom have risen to international fame after their debut with Fiedler. Except for one or two performances at Stern Grove, the concerts are held at Civic Auditorium, where the audience sits at checker-clothed tables on the main floor to enjoy beer and pretzels with their music.

ABUNDANCE *of theatrical activity is offered by the Curran, Geary, and Marines' Memorial Theaters. Pride of the city is the American Conservatory Theater, whose performances prompted one critic to remark, "There is more excitement in a weekend with A.C.T. than an entire month on Broadway."*

Men of the Theater

In its Golden Era, San Francisco not only had its Silver Kings and Railroad Kings, but its Theater Kings as well—impresarios who became as famous as the actors and actresses they presented.

The town's first legitimate theater, the Jenny Lind, was in a loft over Tom Maguire's saloon and gambling hall on Kearny Street near Washington. Maguire could neither read nor write, but he was smart enough to know that Gold Rush communities were starved for entertainment.

Countless fires in the ramshackle town often razed the theaters almost as fast as they were built. Between 1850 and 1860 there were three Jenny Linds, two Americans, two Metropolitans, two Adelphis, and a score of other short-lived theaters. In 1876 Maguire went into partnership with Elias (Lucky) Baldwin, the owner of another theater, the Academy of Music. They built the then-fabulous Baldwin Hotel and Theater on Market and Powell Streets. On opening night, at the Baldwin, the assistant stage manager and prompter was a young man named David Belasco, who later achieved fame as a New York producer but who was always known as a San Francisco boy.

There was money in the theater for Henry "Honest Harry" Meiggs too. The same promoter-swindler-alderman who bilked friends and neighbors out of $1 million and built Meiggs Wharf at the foot of Powell near present-day Fisherman's Wharf, also built the large Music Hall on Bush near Montgomery for concerts, oratorios, lectures, and fairs.

AN ORDERLY and civilized social pattern

CLICK OF DOMINOES and clink of coffee cups are the main sounds emanating from the rooms of the city's clubs. In the words of the Chronicle, *clubs offer a haven of privacy in a world in which it is fast disappearing. A stronghold for men, few clubs admit women except for very special social occasions; one of the city's oldest permitted a female to enter its doors once—on the club's 100th anniversary.*

Signs of Select Socializing

Solidarity, selectivity, and status are reflected in the burnished bronze and polished wood signs that represent the world of private clubs. The aims of clubdom, though springing largely from the desire for social contact, vary from epicurian dining to the furtherance of the arts to sports promotion to all-around enjoyment of good times and comfortable surroundings.

...SELECT SOCIALIZING

GLITTERING seasonal opening at the War Memorial Opera House brings out many of the city's first families, the proceedings traditionally being attended by members of the press in tails. On facing page, mood of mellowed elegance is mirrored in columns flanking entrance to St. Francis Hotel, one of the more fashionable gathering places downtown.

A CITY THAT KNOWS HOW TO RELAX

The Time and the Place to Play

KEEPING THE NOSE TO THE GRINDSTONE is one thing, but—as San Franciscans believe—wearing the proboscis thin is something else. Never having been a place that takes itself too seriously, San Francisco has a history of enjoying life that dates back to the wild Fourth of July celebration thrown by the town's second settler, when the independence of America was commemorated California style.

A vital part of the enjoyment of life is the enjoyment of good food, and San Francisco has a profusion of good food to delight in. The city's mixed background, plus its adventuresome attitude of being willing to try anything, has done much to give it a varied cuisine, and it has just about everything in the way of good eating that anyone could desire.

San Francisco is often called the city that never sleeps. Though official closing time for night spots is 2 A.M., high spirits stay that way well into the wee hours, and many a party has tapered off with guests taking the morning air at Ocean Beach or in one of the city's many parks.

SAN FRANCISCO—the gayest, lightest-hearted, most pleasure-loving city of the Western Continent, is how writer Will Irwin described the city. Its occasional lapses into seriousness are puckishly tempered, and it enjoys the feeling of being as unfettered as the winds that blow through the Golden Gate.

IN SAN FRANCISCO, celebrating is second nature

ANY TIME is a time to celebrate in the city known for its merrymaking. San Francisco Convention and Visitors Bureau makes available a detailed monthly listing of happy events, among which is the Cable Car Bell Ringing Contest held each August in Union Square.

A GIFT BOX with legs, a flower cart with wheels, and a folk singer with guitar are part of the festivities that occur each March in Maiden Lane to celebrate the arrival of spring. Much of the fun is organized, but most of it is spontaneous and contageous.

A PARTY to start all parties, the Fourth of July bash thrown in 1836 by Jacob Leese (the pueblo's second settler) lasted for two days and a night, beginning San Francisco's legend as the city that never sleeps.

CHINATOWN'S LION lunges ferociously at passers-by during local New Year celebration that lasts for several days in late January or February. It takes steady nerves to walk amidst the firecrackers that youths delight in tossing from upper-story windows.

A CITY full of small parks – for fun, or just relaxing

RUMBLE OF TRAFFIC along Post Street is no disturbance at all to a citizen taking his ease behind the hedges of Union Square. Below: Just which of the city's many green spots it is makes little difference; all are fine places for lunching or other noontime activities.

CHESS, CHECKERS, or Chinese chess under the pines is a delightful way to spend an afternoon in Portsmouth Plaza. In 1960 the old, run-down park in the plaza was totally excavated for an underground garage, then rebuilt to form a beautifully landscaped place.

SIGMUND STERN GROVE on Sloat Boulevard draws its greatest crowds during summer concert series, especially for the big jazz festival, which features San Francisco's own Turk Murphy and groups large and small from around the Bay Area.

Box Score of San Francisco Parks

Of San Francisco's 46.6 square miles, 3,575 acres are dedicated to parks and recreation centers. Dotting the city as 140 separate breathing spaces, they range in size from the 1017-acre Golden Gate Park and Panhandle to the tiny public gardens with not more than a bench or two. Following are the ten largest, most-used parks in the city:

Name	Principal Use	Location	Acres
Aquatic Park	Fishing	Polk & Beach Streets	31
Fleishhacker Playground	Zoo/Play	Great Highway & Sloat Boulevard	146
Golden Gate Park & Panhandle	General	Ocean Beach to Baker Street	1017
Great Highway/Ocean Beach	Beach	Great Highway Parkway	140
Lake Merced & Harding Park	Fishing/Golf	Skyline & Harding Boulevards	700
Lincoln Park	Museum/Golf	34th Avenue and Clement Street	193
McLaren Park	General	McLaren Park Road	318
Palace of Fine Arts	Open Space	Marina & Lyon Streets	16
Pine Lake Park	Open Space	Crestlake Drive & Vale Street	31
Stern Grove	Concerts	19th Avenue & Sloat Boulevard	33

Open spaces also appear in such green spots as Chinatown's Portsmouth Plaza, the city's first plaza, and downtown Union Square. Other green areas include Mission Dolores Park, Washington Park, St. Mary's Square, Balboa Park, Mountain Lake Park, Yacht Harbor, Alta Plaza Park, Bay View Park, Duboce Park, Parkside Square, Huntington Park, Civic Center Plaza, Garfield Square, and numerous recreation centers and playgrounds. Particularly good spots for a view are Buena Vista Hill, Coolbrith Square, Mount Davidson, Fort Funston, Glen Park Canyon, Mount Olympus, Telegraph Hill, Twin Peaks, and Sutro Heights.

...THE SMALL PARKS

A PLACE OF ROLLING HILLS and windswept open spaces, John McLaren Park offers views of the city's northern edge on one side, of Visitacion Valley and the San Bruno Mountains on the other. One of the few city parks in a natural state, its slopes of wild barley and oats surround clusters of eucalyptus, Monterey cypress, and Monterey pine.

HOW TO MAKE the most of a most pleasant leisure

IN THIS CITY of concentrated population, pursuits of ease are wonderfully numerous and diverse, and people don't find time for fun—they make *time. The workaday world may be a necessity, but it certainly isn't an obsession for San Franciscans; an hour or an afternoon can always be put to good use in just poking along the shore to discover what treasures have been washed up by the sea. Bakers Beach, outside Golden Gate Bridge, is a beachcomber's happy hunting grounds.*

WHEN the stripers are running in the bay (June, July, August), fishermen get there even if it means donning a rubber suit against the icy water. Favorite spots for surf casting are Ocean Beach, Phelan State Beach, Bakers Beach. Inside the Gate there are more rocks to snag a line, but that's little deterrent to anglers at Fort Point, the Marina Green, and Aquatic Park Pier.

WHAT BETTER WAY to spend a lunch break downtown than reading in Zellerbach Plaza. On sunny days office workers relax in the park-like surroundings by listening to occasional concerts or by sitting on "the wall" where they can see and be seen. The stores are an invitation to a little shopping, but when the weather is good there's always tomorrow.

...MAKING THE MOST OF LEISURE

THERE ARE WORSE WAYS to whittle down a morning than a friendly game of cards. Perhaps one of these denizens of North Beach started out on an errand of vast import, but apparently he became distracted by more urgent matters. Seldom hurried, San Franciscans get things done but in their own way and in their own time.

LEISURE on a large scale is manifest at the Cow Palace, a huge building that derives its unlovely name from being the home of the Grand National livestock exposition. Although just out of the county limits, the Palace is part and parcel of San Francisco. When residents refer to "the Palace," other locals instinctively know whether they mean the Cow Palace, the Sheraton-Palace Hotel, the Palace of the Legion of Honor, or the Palace of Fine Arts.

STREET MUSICIANS *play for pay but mostly for pleasure at spontaneous sidewalk concerts. Impromptu performances throughout the city feature anything from classical to bluegrass. Reflecting the city's casual outdoor life style, artists prefer simple, carefree attire over conventional concert garb. Most street musicians are dedicated and serious, serenading their appreciative audiences with virtuoso performances on instruments ranging from baroque flutes to miniature harpsichords.*

AFTER DARK, life begins all over again

CLICHES ABOUND when it comes to describing San Francisco, but one that fits like a glove is "The city that never sleeps." Lively enough by day, the city becomes increasingly animated with the onset of evening. Broadway (above) means the same in San Francisco as it does in New York: bright lights, restaurants, theaters, and nightlife.

NOT ALL OPERA is at the Opera House, and not all Greek dancers are in Athens. The Bocce Ball, an institution in North Beach, features operatic arias during which the entire audience occasionally provides a less-professional yet enthusiastic chorus. Patrons of Greek tavernas have been known, in their enthusiasm, to join the costumed dancers.

...AFTER DARK

AFTER the excitement of the early evening has died down, it's time for a breather. A couple shares quiet conversation over Irish coffee behind the tree-framed window of the Buena Vista's back room.

A CONSUMING interest in good food

FLOCKED WALLPAPER and converted gaslights set the Victorian decor at Giovanni's, one of many family style Italian restaurants where Father serves soup and salad at the table and where courses run from relishes to soup to salad to pasta to entrée to dessert—and thence to satiation.

INTO THE PAN go paper-thin slices of beef, fresh mushrooms, soy sauce, and other delectable ingredients of sukiyaki. Part of the fun in dining at a Japanese restaurant is in watching the waitress prepare the meal right at the table.

Good Food-A Tradition of Variety and Diversity

*International influences have been at work in the city's kitchens
since the days of the Gold Rush when Frenchmen, Chinese, and Germans
flocked ashore from early sailing ships. Over the years the
Italians, Armenians, Basques, Indians, Mexicans, Russians, Spanish,
and Scandinavians have added their contributions. In San Francisco
there is no feeling of affectation when you speak French or Greek or
Japanese to a waiter—it's part of the city's international variety.*

Foods of San Francisco

San Franciscans have always been interested in a variety of foods, and local chefs have developed numerous original creations. Here are just three of San Francisco's many famous recipes:

CELERY VICTOR

Chef Victor Hirtzler of the St. Francis Hotel originated this classic in the early 1900's.

    2 small hearts of celery
    1 medium-sized onion
    2½ cups bouillon or chicken stock
    1 cup well-seasoned French dressing
       Watercress or shredded lettuce
       Coarsely ground black pepper
       Anchovy fillets
       Pimiento strips
       Fresh tomatoes (optional)
       Ripe olives (optional)

Wash celery, trim root end, and cut off all but smallest leaves. Peel and slice onion. Put whole celery hearts and sliced onion in shallow pan; cover with bouillon. Cover and cook until tender, about 15 minutes. Let cool in stock. Remove hearts, cut in half lengthwise, and place in shallow dish. Pour over French dressing and chill several hours.

To serve, drain off most of the dressing and place celery on watercress or shredded lettuce. Sprinkle with pepper and garnish with anchovy fillets and pimiento strips. Tomatoes and ripe olives may be used for extra garnish.

SHELLFISH CIOPPINO

No one really knows for sure where cioppino got its name or when it was created. But San Francisco's Italian families knew the dish well at the beginning of the century.

    1 large onion, sliced
    1 bunch green onions, including part of the
       tops, sliced
    1 green pepper, seeded and diced
    2 whole large cloves garlic
    ⅓ cup olive oil or salad oil
    ⅓ cup chopped parsley
    1 can (1 lb.) tomato purée
    1 can (8 oz.) tomato sauce
       Tomato sauce can of white or red table wine,
       or water
       Tomato purée can of water
       Half a bay leaf
    3 teaspoons salt
    ¼ teaspoon pepper
    ⅛ teaspoon *each* rosemary and thyme
    2 medium-sized Dungeness crabs
    1 dozen fresh clams in shells
    1 pound fresh prawns or large shrimp in shells

In a Dutch oven or a frying pan that has a cover, sauté onion, green onion, green pepper, and garlic in olive oil about 5 minutes. Add parsley, tomato purée, tomato sauce, wine, and water (or use all water), and all seasonings. Cover and simmer about an hour. Remove garlic.

Clean and crack live Dungeness crabs, or have this done at the fish market; arrange crab pieces in bottom of a large pan (at least 8-quart size). Scrub clams well and put in on top of crab. Cut shrimp or prawns down backs with kitchen scissors, then wash out sand veins; put on top of clams. Pour on hot prepared sauce, cover, and simmer until clam shells open, 20 to 30 minutes.

Serve in large soup bowls or soup plates, with some of each shellfish in each bowl. Makes about 6 servings. Sourdough French bread and a green salad are good accompaniments.

GREEN GODDESS

First created at the Palace Hotel in 1915 and named after a play titled "The Green Goddess," this salad is still a popular luncheon entrée at the present Sheraton-Palace.

    8 to 10 anchovy fillets
    1 green onion
    ¼ cup minced parsley
    2 tablespoons minced fresh tarragon or 1 table-
       spoon dried tarragon soaked in vinegar and
       then strained
    ¼ cup finely cut chives
    3 cups mayonnaise
    ¼ cup tarragon vinegar
    1 clove garlic
    1 large head romaine
    1 pound cooked lobster, shrimp, crab meat, or
       chicken

Chop together anchovies and green onion until finely minced. Add parsley, tarragon, and chives, and mix lightly. Turn into a bowl and stir in mayonnaise and vinegar, mixing well. Rub a salad bowl with 1 cut clove of garlic and break romaine into bite-sized pieces into the bowl.

Pour over enough dressing to moisten (about 2 cups), toss lightly, spoon on salad plates, and garnish with desired shellfish or chicken. Serves 6. Recipe makes about 1 quart dressing.

...GOOD FOOD

CLIPPER RESTAURANT
Nos. 311 and 313 Pacific Street.
GEORGE W. DETTNER
PROPRIETOR & MANAGER

BREAKFAST AND SUPPER.

COOKED TO ORDER.

Porterhouse Steak..............20	Tenderloin Steak..............20
Sirloin Steak..............15	Veal Cutlets, plain or
Rib Steak..............15	breaded..............10
Beefsteak, Spanish style..10	Ham, fried or broiled..10
Beefsteak, plain..............10	Bacon..............10
Pork Chops..............10	Tripe, stewed..............10
Mutton Chops..............10	Domestic Sausages.......10
Stewed Beef and Onions.10	Cold Meats..............10
Stewed Veal..............10	Corn Beef Hash..............10
Fish Stew..............10	Cold Boiled Ham..............10
Fried Liver with Pork...10	
Pig's Feet in batter.......10	
Mackerel, boiled or broiled..............10	
Tripe in batter..............10	
Salmon, fried or broiled.10	
Hamburg Beefsteak..............10	
Pig's Feet, soused..........10	
Stewed Mutton..............10	

EGGS AND OYSTERS.

3 Fried Eggs..............15	Omelette, 3 Eggs..............15	Oyster Stew..............20
3 Boiled Eggs..............15	Ham and 2 Eggs..............15	
3 Scrambled Eggs..............15	Bacon and 2 Eggs..............15	

HOT CAKES.

German Pan Cakes..............15
Dry Toast..............5
Milk, or Boston Cream Toast..............10
Bowl of Milk, with Mush or Bread..............10
Black Tea, Coffee or Glass of Milk..............5
Hot Cakes, Flannel Cakes and Corn Batter..............5
Chocolate..............10

DINNER.

SOUPS.

Chicken..............5 | Potato..............5

All 15 Cent Orders and upwards will be served with Butter free of charge. Bread and Potatoes with Meats and Fish free of charge. All single 5 Cent dishes, 10 Cents.

FISH.

Salt Codfish, Family..............10	Salmon, baked or fried..10
Bass, baked or fried..............10	Mackerel..............10
Fried Tomcods..............10	
Fried Smelts..............10	

BOILED.

Mutton, Mint Sauce..............10	Corn Beef and Cabbage..10
Pig's Head..............10	Corned Pork " ..10
Calf's " Pickle Sauce..10	Ham..............10
Calf Tongue..............10	
Boiled Beef..............10	

ROASTS.

Beef, stuffed or plain..............10	Mutton..............10
Veal..............10	Pork..............10
Roast Mutton, Mint Sauce.10	
Chicken..............20	

ENTRIES.

Roast Pork and Sauer-kraut..............10	Veal Pot Pie..............10
Sour Beef..............10	Beefsteak Pie..............10
	Lamb Chops..............10
Beef, Spanish style..............10	
Stewed Kidney..............10	
Beef a la Mode..............10	

*Special today [handwritten:] Calf's Head Spanish 10¢
Fried Shrimp in Batter 10¢
Assorted Cold Meats — 15¢
Veal Chops in Batter — 10¢*

PUDDINGS.	PIES.	CAKES.
Corn Starch..............5	Apple..............5	Doughnuts..............5
Rice..............5	Peach..............5	Pound Cake..............5
Tapioca..............5	Cranberry..............5	
Sago..............5		

WINES AND LIQUORS.

California Claret..............20	White Wine..............25	Glass of Beer..............5
Half Bottle..............10	Ale and Porter, bottle..15	

Dispute with waiter or dissatisfaction must be settled at the Bar.

Credit in all Cases Positively Declined.

PREOCCUPATION *with fine fare dates back to late 1800's when veal chops in batter and calf's head "Spanish" were offered as the day's special . . . at a dime each.*

NOT EVEN IN FRANCE *is French bread as crusty and as sour as it is in San Francisco. Loaves ranging in shape from flat to round to long to very long are sold in hotel lobbies and at the airport to enable departing visitors to take with them a fond memory of the city. The scored crust facilitates tearing apart a loaf the traditional way.*

Creating New Vitality from Old Forms

LET OTHER CITIES tear down the old to make way for the new—let other cities sneer at their adolescence as something to be left behind, something that's better rid of. Though not all residents of the city by the Golden Gate are vitally aware of the place's rich history, most are quick to cry out in protest if a time-worn landmark is in danger of being destroyed in the name of progress.

San Francisco holds its customs and traditions high and fashions its growth to fit them. Hardly a day goes by that the mayor or board of supervisors or planning commission isn't set upon by organized opposition to the destruction of the city's past. A case in point is the Sea Wall, a onetime brick warehouse near the Embarcadero. Doomed, along with several other buildings that were on the site of a new development, the Sea Wall was slated to come down in 1969 under the wrecker's ball. But on the day that demolition was to begin, a group of ladies barricaded themselves in the building, waving banners and shouting slogans. The destruction contractor finally gave in and an agreement was reached whereby that at least the brick façade of the building would be preserved until a decision could be reached on how to affect a permanent preservation of that bit of the past.

OLD BRICK is combined with concrete walkways and open escalators at The Cannery, a revitalized fruit packing plant dating to pre-earthquake days. Arched windows preserve Victorian past in a setting housing ultra-modern shops.

AN EXUBERANT CITY

INDIVIDUAL EFFORTS to preserve the character of the past

FEW OTHER CITIES allow themselves to become so enamored of parts of the past that citizens zealously seek out old-time firehouses to be turned into charming dwellings.

DEBATE-PROVOKING point is whether bay windows were originally devised to form a recess in a room or to give a half-circle view of the bay of San Francisco. A house without bay windows is often just another house, but one with them is San Francisco personified.

FRENCH MAILBOX
*surmounted by gorgeously
crested initials, a large gas lamp,
and an ornate door lintel mark
the entrance to offices of
attorney Melvin Belli on
Montgomery Street. Through the
doorway is a charming courtyard
graced by iron work, plantings,
and old brick.*

...PRESERVING THE PAST

HISTORY IS PRESERVED along Union Street west of Van Ness. In the post-Gold Rush days the area was part of Cow Hollow, a green section of the city where herds of dairy cattle grazed. The carriage houses, cow barns, and Victorian houses were much too valuable a part of the city's past to be allowed to slip into oblivion, so imaginative individuals converted many of the old places as tributes to nostalgia.

The Past that's Best Left in Limbo

The gold-hungry adventurers and the land-starved sailors who reached San Francisco in the mid-1880's were ready to let loose. And release was easy to find.

Some men found it on the Barbary Coast, six or eight waterfront blocks of honky-tonks, saloons, and cheap lodging houses along Pacific, Broadway, and Kearny Streets (now Jackson Square). But since few seamen were willing to rejoin their ships, a method of forceful recruitment—called shanghaiing—became a profitable business there. Runners would meet the ships and lure their quarries to dives and boardinghouses with promises of liquid refreshment and revelry. There, the sailors would be rapped on the head with a bung starter and dropped through a trapdoor into a row boat for delivery back to the docks.

Barbarous as the Coast used to be, Morton Street was said to be worse. Police seldom entered the two-block stretch between Kearny and Stockton unless compelled to by a murder, shooting, or stabbing. It took the fire of 1906 to purge the alley, which was subsequently renamed Union Square Avenue, Manila Avenue, and, finally, in 1922, Maiden Lane. Now a sedate pedestrian-way off Union Square, the fashionable shopping lane gives no hint of its lurid past.

In nearby Chinatown, the warrens of Waverly Place held an estimated 2,000 Chinese slave girls and Dupont Street (now Grant Avenue) held girls of other nationalities. The first of San Francisco's tong wars erupted on Waverly in 1875 over ownership of a girl, and the last was in 1926.

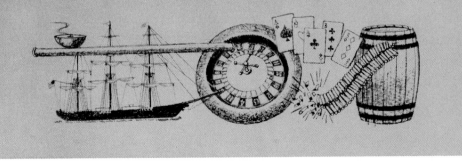

THE CHOCOLATE FACTORY that became
a lively institution

GHIRARDELLI SQUARE, one-time woolen works and later a chocolate factory, is one of the most pleasurable places in the city. Overlooking San Francisco Maritime Historical Park (at left) and Aquatic Park, the miscellany of brick structures bears such captivating names as Mustard Building, Power House, Woolen Mill, Cocoa Building. Of the shops, galleries, theaters, restaurants, and plazas, perhaps the happiest place of all is the old-time ice cream parlor where a limited amount of the rich chocolate is still made in the manner of yesterday and where goggle-eyed children consume sundaes large enough to founder a hungry adult.

TILE ROOFS were not part of the original architectural style, but as elements of new additions they are instrumental in bringing even more warmth to the surroundings. Flower beds, trees, benches, and tables with bright umbrellas all invite visitors to relax and enjoy. The concrete pillars are part of the Ghirardelli bookstore, where browsers crowd each other cozily between well stocked racks. On the level just below the second railing is a close-to-life-sized stone bear with his nose pointing bayward—a creation of Benny Bufano.

SOMETIMES CONTROVERSIAL mermaid fountain, designed by Ruth Asawa, is a sparkling focal point of the Square and an ideal meeting place. Past the olive trees is the Wurster Building, named after the architect who remodeled the complex.

...GHIRARDELLI SQUARE

BENEFACTOR for this cheerful center was William Roth, a steamship magnate, who feared that if the Ghirardelli buildings were not preserved they would be replaced by a view-spoiling group of high-rise apartments. He bought the place and financed its renovation, preserving the original form but adding to it in similar architectural style. The clock tower houses the studios of a radio station whose call letters are, appropriately, KFOG.

YOU CAN take an elevator up, but why ride when the outside stairway between the Cocoa and Mustard Buildings gives such a fine view of the main plaza. Diners are on the terrace of Sea Witch restaurant, which adjoins Portofino Caffe, the place to go in the square if you're in the mood for a cup of very black and very thick espresso.

THE CANNERY—smart shops in a setting of old brick

RED BRICK MAZE on Leavenworth, between Fisherman's Wharf and Ghirardelli Square, was a fruit cannery around the turn of the century. Today the cans are gone but the ground-floor market that opens onto Jefferson offers an array of exotic fruits, as well as cheeses and wines . . . plus French bread flown over from Paris—which, of course, doesn't hold a candle to San Francisco's own. The market is but one of a grand selection of shops and restaurants adding new vitality to an old property.

SPACES BETWEEN BUILDINGS at The Cannery are as important as the spaces within. The flower filled courtyards are a delight to strollers, who gather to listen to a folk singer or just take their ease in the sunshine. The concourse is shaded by full-sized olive trees, transplanted from northern California, that are strung with tiny lights hardly visible during the day but which make the place a fairyland after dark. The Cannery's star-in-a-circle trademark is taken from the old metal tie plates used in brick wall construction.

OLD FORMS . . . NEW VITALITY **215**

THE NORTH WATERFRONT – growing record of a seafaring heritage

BALCLUTHA *sits resignedly at Pier 43 mooring, hard by Fisherman's Wharf and in view of Telegraph Hill, where a semaphore used to notify the town of ships entering the bay. The metal-hulled square-rigger is a floating museum and a colorful reminder of San Francisco's seafaring past.*

"WHAT'S DOWN THERE?" youngsters want to know when they peer through the hatch grating of C. A. Thayer, *an old schooner kept trim and neat at the Hyde Street Pier ship museum.* Thayer *served as a coastal lumber carrier and an Alaskan fishing vessel before sailing to home port in 1957. She's berthed in the company of the scow schooner* Alma, *the steam schooner* Wapama, *and the ferry* Eureka. *It's a quiet retirement for the salt-water veterans.*

THE NORTH WATERFRONT

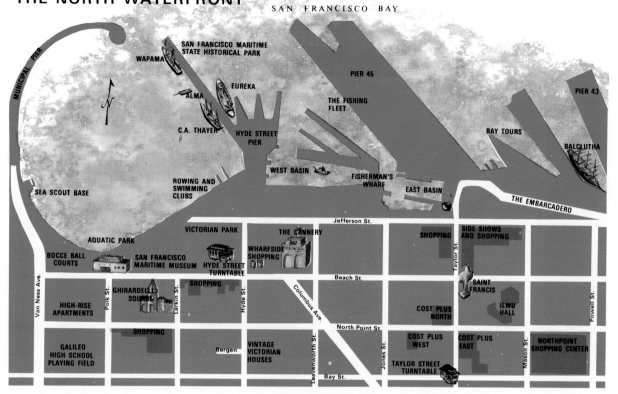

SAN FRANCISCO BAY

MUNICIPAL PIER

SAN FRANCISCO MARITIME STATE HISTORICAL PARK

WAPAMA

ALMA

EUREKA

C.A. THAYER

HYDE STREET PIER

PIER 45

THE FISHING FLEET

PIER 43

BAY TOURS

BALCLUTHA

WEST BASIN

FISHERMAN'S WHARF

EAST BASIN

THE EMBARCADERO

SEA SCOUT BASE

ROWING AND SWIMMING CLUBS

AQUATIC PARK

VICTORIAN PARK

THE CANNERY

Jefferson St.

SHOPPING

SIDE SHOWS AND SHOPPING

BOCCE BALL COURTS

SAN FRANCISCO MARITIME MUSEUM

HYDE STREET TURNTABLE

WHARFSIDE SHOPPING

Beach St.

Taylor St.

SAINT FRANCIS

ILWU HALL

Van Ness Ave.

Polk St.

GHIRARDELLI SQUARE

Larkin St.

SHOPPING

Hyde St.

Columbus Ave.

North Point St.

COST PLUS NORTH

Powell St.

HIGH-RISE APARTMENTS

SHOPPING

Bergen

VINTAGE VICTORIAN HOUSES

Leavenworth St.

Jones St.

COST PLUS WEST

COST PLUS EAST

Mason St.

NORTHPOINT SHOPPING CENTER

GALILEO HIGH SCHOOL PLAYING FIELD

Bay St.

TAYLOR STREET TURNTABLE

UNTIL MID-1950, most visitors to the industrial north waterfront came to see the boats at Fisherman's Wharf or to dine in one of the Wharf's seafood restaurants. Today this district contains a growing collection of old sailing vessels that is equaled only at Mystic Seaport, Connecticut; it has one of the country's best maritime museums; and it is a center of major drawing power because of its shopping complexes, theaters, and restaurants.

WORKING END of Fisherman's Wharf is a place of high adventure for lads who like the smell of the sea. When not clattering along the back wharf, they're to be found watching commercial fishermen ready their boats for the next day or gazing wistfully at the big freighters crowded up to the docks to discharge cargo.

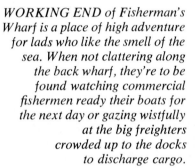

OPEN-MOUTH AWE is a silent compliment to the fine collections of yesteryear at San Francisco's Maritime Museum. Beautiful ship models share space with anchors, figureheads, and other objects of maritime lore, as well as an excellent collection of photographs that re-live the history of the San Francisco waterfront. The boat-shaped concrete building housing the museum, along with a senior citizen's center, was originally built as a casino.

...THE NORTH WATERFRONT

FISHERMAN'S WHARF still remains one of the city's major visitor attractions and is a favorite of residents, even though most wouldn't admit to succumbing to the lure of such a tourist center. The Wharf is built near the site of Harry Meiggs' long wharf . . . "Honest" Harry Meiggs, as he was known in the mid-1800's, before people learned that he had embezzled some $800,000 in city funds and absconded to South America. The popularity of the Wharf grew from the practice of fishermen selling their catch fresh from the boat and the subsequent establishment of many seafood restaurants. Two meal-time favorites reputed to have originated here are the "Walkaway Cocktail"—shrimp or crab with sauce in a paper cup, to be consumed while strolling—and Crab Louis (pronounced Looey), a man-sized salad of crab meat covered with Thousand Island dressing.

MONUMENT to "one of the greatest fairs ever"

OPENING OF PANAMA CANAL was celebrated in San Francisco by the Pan Pacific Exposition of 1915 (see below), built on reclaimed land that is today part of the Marina. Twenty-five nations and 43 states and territories contributed to the fair. One of the grandest buildings was the Palace of Fine Arts, designed by Bernard Maybeck to resemble a Roman ruin. The structure on Baker Street was saved from destruction when the rest of the fair was razed, but it crumbled into a genuine ruin over the years. In 1958 local businessman Walter Johnson donated more than $2 million to restore the Palace; this plus other donations and allocations by the city gave San Francisco another permanent landmark.

STROLLING through the magnificent temple is like taking a step into a long-past golden age. One of the favored spots of sentimental San Franciscans, the Marina's Palace of Fine Arts (not to be confused with the Palace of the Legion of Honor) was reconstructed at a cost ten times that of the original. Though the place has no practical use, it has been called an unprecedented civic investment in pure aesthetics which may never again be matched.

THE FORT that guards the Golden Gate

PRESIDIO OF SAN FRANCISCO is a command center for military activities in the eight Far Western states. In its northernmost corner, half-hidden under the Golden Gate Bridge, is Fort Point (officially called Fort Winfield Scott). Built in 1861 along the lines of Fort Sumter, it is a classic example of the brick forts constructed in the 1800's to guard the United States seacoast. During World Wars I and II, German prisoners were housed within its walls and a small gun battery was stationed here. For years the foreboding-looking place was used by the presidio and by other agencies for a storage area and its exterior was known only to fishermen or persons curious enough to find their way down to water's edge under the southern arch of the bridge.

TODAY, Fort Point is open to the public on Saturdays and Sundays from 1 to 4 P.M. (To reach it, turn off Lincoln Boulevard in the presidio at Long Avenue, proceed to Marine Drive, and turn left.) Interior courtyard is half the size of a football field, and from it visitors can inspect the impressively solid construction. Bricks in the arched galleries (see above right) were made on Russian Hill and at San Quentin; granite came from China. The iron-studded door, above, leads to a small prison cell block. At present writing there are plans for turning Fort Point into a military museum containing relics of four wars: Civil, Indian, Spanish-American, and the Philippine Insurrection.

LONG HAUL UP HYDE STREET peaks on Russian Hill, as car clatters across Lombard (called the crookedest street in the world). Look to the east for an eye-level view of Telegraph Hill and Coit Tower, to the west for a quick glimpse of the Marina, the presidio, and Golden Gate Bridge. Though they may act blasé about it, San Franciscans know that the best seats on the cable car are the outside ones, where you can really see the city, as well as watch the gripman in action.

A NATIONAL LANDMARK that goes
nine miles an hour

SHOWMAN INCARNATE, the gripman keeps up a rapid-fire flow of shouted instructions— ranging from "Hang on for the curve!" to "Step back in the car!" — all accompanied by a personalized rhythm embroidered on the bell. When he hauls back on the grip handle, unwary passengers standing behind are likely to get a solid elbow in the ribs, but it's passed off in good nature. Camaraderie that centers around the cable cars hadn't yet evolved when the picture below was taken of the original Clay Street Line.

THAT LITTLE SLOT IN THE STREET has a cable running below it, and that cable can become a nightmare of a snarl if it has to be fished out of the slot. Although the cable and its accompanying hardware are kept under constant surveillance and are carefully maintained, the wire rope on occasion will become frayed or snagged. If the trouble isn't spotted at the powerhouse (located at Washington and Mason), it may require a crew to pry up the cable and repair the damage on the spot. Beauty may be lost on the workmen, but the tracks and switching hardware create unique and interesting patterns in the street.

How a Cable Car Works

San Francisco is the only city in the world with an operating cable car system. And so beloved is it, by both natives and visitors, that in 1964 the U.S. Interior Department's National Park Service declared the cable cars a National Historic Landmark.

Legend has it that Andrew Smith Hallidie, a London-born engineer, was moved to invent the cable system by compassion for the beasts that supplied the power for the old horse cars. The story goes that in 1869 he watched a team of four horses struggling on slippery cobbles to haul a fully laden car up a steep hill. When one horse fell, the car rolled back, dragging all four horses behind it. Hallidie vowed to put a stop to such cruelty and, with his partners, built the Clay Street Railroad Company.

In brief, the mechanical process is as follows: A continuous steel cable, which provides the motive power for all the cars, runs in a slot 18 inches below the surface of the street. This 1¼-inch wire rope travels 840 feet a minute, or about nine miles per hour, and is driven by 12-foot winding wheels turned by an electric motor in the central carbarn.

The connection between the cars and the running cable is a pincer-like device called a grip, which is fastened to the forward truck of the car and extends down through a slot in the street to the cable. When the gripman pulls the lever back, pressure is put on the cable and the car is put in motion slowly. When he pulls the lever completely back, the car moves forward at nine miles per hour.

Back in 1880 there were eight lines with 112 miles of track criss-crossing the steep hills of San Francisco. Now only 17 miles of track remain, and the total system has been reduced to 39 cars —27 "single-enders" on the two Powell Street routes and 12 "double-enders" on the California Street run. (The single type has turntables at each end of the line, while the double type switches on a "Y" at each end.)

Little has dimmed the popularity of the city's cable cars. Every now and then someone makes suggestions regarding more efficient modes of transportation, but the resulting public clamor can be heard around the world. In 1947 members of a San Francisco citizen's committee resolved to "Save the Cable Cars" and put the issue on a ballot. Save them they did. Now there is a provision in the city charter that guarantees perpetuation of the three remaining lines. And during the peak of the summer season the cable cars continue to carry as many as 25,000 passengers a day.

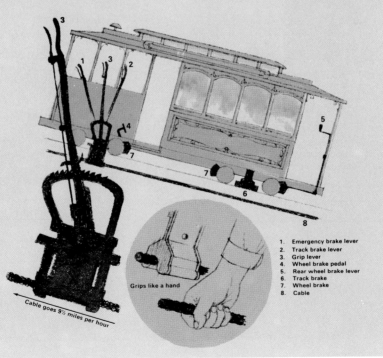

Grips like a hand

Cable goes 9½ miles per hour

1. Emergency brake lever
2. Track brake lever
3. Grip lever
4. Wheel brake pedal
5. Rear wheel brake lever
6. Track brake
7. Wheel brake
8. Cable

STALKING the Victorians – a favorite pastime

PRESERVATION of historic buildings is not unique to San Francisco (New Orleans, Boston, and Philadelphia have protected sectors of old structures), but San Franciscans are unequaled in attachment to their gingerbread palaces. In virtually every district of the city are blocks of Victorians, many of them restored to face-scrubbed newness, most of them proudly occupied by individuals happy to retain this intimate touch with the city's past.

LAGUNA STREET, in its 1800 block, has many homes built between 1885 and 1890 that have been lovingly refurbished by their owners to preserve the early San Francisco flavor. The fronts are a mixture of fine detailing that was the style of the times.

...THE VICTORIANS

GABLE WINDOW

SLANTED BAY

WITCH'S HAT TURRET

OEIL DE BOEUF WINDOW WITH CARTOUCHE

CUPOLA

GAZEBO

CONTRAST of light and dark so characteristic of San Francisco is epitomized in façades of its old homes (houses above are in 2000 block of Pierce Street). The city's Victorians are characterized by towers, columned porches, wooden filigree, stained glass, and bay windows. Drawing illustrates some of the more common architectural elements.

A Guide to the Victorians

MISSION DISTRICT

Guerrero Street, from 800 block to 1500 block
Italianate, Queen Anne, Stick; several interesting examples of ornate frieze. (In 1886, a Captain A. Dodd ferried lumber for his house, number 1325, to San Francisco aboard his own ship.)

Dolores Street, 700–1500
Stick, Italianate. (In 1879 a Charles Katz purchased number 1202, then a one-room shack; in 1909 he incorporated the original dwelling in a new house built in the Queen Anne tradition.)

Sanchez Street, 300–1700
Stick, Italianate. (Number 775–77, built in 1904 of shingles and wood, is known as the first residence on Sanchez Hill.)

Noe Street, 300–1600
Italianate, Stick—many with ornate detailing. (Numbers 344–46 are good examples of Italianate, while numbers 437–39 are representative of Stick.)

20th, 21st, 22nd, 23rd Streets, 3000–4000
Nearly 40 square blocks containing many fine examples of elaborate Stick, grand Italianate, Queen Anne. (Chemical Company #44 used number 3816 22nd, built in 1910, as its firehouse for over fifty years, when the structure was converted into a residence.)

PACIFIC HEIGHTS

Vallejo Street, 1600–2900
Queen Anne, Stick; some good examples of Baroque Revival and Tudor Revival. (Ephraim Willard Burr, one of San Francisco's early mayors, had number 1772 built as a wedding gift for his son in 1875.)

Broadway, 1700–2900
Good variety of Italianate, Stick, Queen Anne, Colonial Revival, Georgian Revival, Dutch Colonial. (The private school for girls at number 2120 is a former residence of James Flood, the Comstock silver king.)

Pacific Avenue, 1800–3500
Several Queen Anne, several Georgian and Classic Revival, some fine shingled houses.

Jackson Street, 1100–3800
Twenty-seven blocks of Italianate, Queen Anne, Stick; several striking examples of Classic Revival.

Washington Street, 2100–3900
Eighteen blocks of Italianate, Stick, Queen Anne.

Pierce Street, 1900–2700
Queen Anne, Stick, Italianate. (Number 2727 was once the grand manor house of Cow Hollow.)

Scott Street, 1900–3000
Stick, Italianate. (Number 2710 was designed in 1893 by Willis Polk, noted architect around the turn of the century.)

Divisadero Street, 1900–2700
Stick, Italianate; several good examples of turret gable bay windows. (Constructed in 1874, numbers 2229 and 2231 were later purchased and remodeled by Julia Morgan, a San Francisco architect and the designer of William Randolph Hearst's San Simeon.)

RUSSIAN HILL

Green Street, 700–1900
Wide variety of Queen Anne; Italianate apartments; several interesting approaches to shingling.

Vallejo Street, 1000 Block
The only area of frame construction surrounded by the 1906 fire that survived. (Numbers 1013–1015–1017 were the home of the architect Willis Polk.)

Russian Hill Place
Numbers 1, 3, 5, and 7, in the tiled-roof Mediterranean style, were designed in 1915 by Willis Polk.

WESTERN ADDITION

Clay Street, 2400–3900
Wide range of Italianate and Stick; many good examples of Period and Queen Anne detailing. (Number 3362 is a four-story Georgian Revival, designed by Willis Polk in 1896.)

Sacramento Street, 1100–3400
Stick, Italianate; several good examples of French Baroque Revival at numbers 1242 and 2151.

California Street, 1800–3000
Mostly Italianate, with some Stick.

Pine Street, 1800–3000
Wide range of Italianate, Stick. (Three interesting Italianate homes are together at numbers 2018, 2020, and 2022.)

Bush Street, 1600–2900
Good range of Italianate, Queen Anne, Stick; some Classic Revival apartments. (Number 2006, a Victorian Gothic, was built around 1852 and has remained in the same family ever since.)

Sutter Street, 1400–2700
Italianate, Stick; some good examples of Queen Anne. (Number 1815, built in 1878, belonged to Captain and Mrs. John Cavarly, subjects of Kathryn Hulme's *Annie's Captain.*)

Post Street, 1300–2600
Good examples of mixed Queen Anne and Italianate styles (number 1406–08 is one); several flat-fronted Italianates; some Stick.

Laguna Street, 1600–3000
Chiefly Italianate.

Buchanan Street, 1700–2600
Italianate (several fine examples), Stick, Queen Anne. (The handsome brick building at 3640 was headquarters of San Francisco Gas Company.)

Webster Street, 1700–3000
Italianate, Stick, Queen Anne. (Worth noting is the unusual Vedanta Temple at number 2963.)

Steiner Street, 1800–3000
Italianate, Stick; several good examples of Queen Anne.

Baker Street, 1400–2100
Flat-front Italianate, Stick, a few Colonial Revivals. (Numbers 1902, 1905, 1906, 1907, and 1909—all one-story cottages—are said to have been built by the father of Oscar Lewis, noted San Francisco writer.)

Architectural Fashions and Forms

Queen Anne. A style prevailing in England in the 1860's that combines classical designs with medieval, 18th-century, and Japanese motifs; characterized by rounded corner towers, shingles, and combinations of posts or rails with brick or other material.

Stick. A version of Victorian employing structural formulas of Sir Charles Locke Eastlake, English architect; characterized by squared bay windows and ornately decorative brackets.

Italianate. Conforming to style prevalent in Italy from Renaissance to 17th century; characterized by slanted bay windows, fanciful pediments crowning a colonnade, a sense of mass.

Georgian. A distinctive national style prevalent in England in 1702-1830; characterized by deep front or side porches, Palladian windows (arched opening flanked by two smaller, square-headed openings).

The Dynamics of Enterprise

THE QUICKEST WAY TO GET RESULTS in San Francisco is to tell a San Franciscan that there is something he is unable to do. This is tantamount to hitting him in the face with a glove, for you have not only thrown out a challenge, you have made it a matter of honor, and the San Franciscan will-by-God do whatever it is you have dared him to do if he has to move the earth to do it.

The city's people like challenges because they are used to them. The earthquake and fire of 1906 posed one of the greatest—that of rebuilding the place after it had been virtually destroyed—and San Franciscans have been taking up the gauntlet ever since.

The city's location itself is a challenge. Being isolated by water on three sides has posed considerable problems. Nature conspires to whittle away the landscape, and not a few answers have had to be found in combatting friendly yet relentless forces of the elements. And no problem ever topped that of connecting San Francisco with the cities and communities across the bay. This challenge was met and conquered in two stages—completion of the Golden Gate Bridge and the Bay Bridge.

GOLDEN GATE BRIDGE *was constructed where everyone said a bridge couldn't be built, in the face of enormous opposition that was both natural and man-made. The net slung under the traffic deck between the two towers for the safety of bridge workers is similar to the one used during construction.*

GREAT HIGHWAY–a playground at ocean's edge

PACIFIC COMBERS and vicious current make Ocean Beach a dangerous place to swim, yet thousands are drawn here and to Playland, a Coney Island type of amusement park on the east side of Great Highway. For years the city's western shore was constantly being nibbled away by the sea until John McLaren, "father of Golden Gate Park," determinedly compacted brush along much of the beach to keep the sand in place. In later years concrete piling, extending 13 feet below extreme low tide, stabilized the roadway.

CHILDREN'S ZOO is by far the most popular part of San Francisco Zoological Gardens—a long name for a superb collection of animals from the world over. Youngsters are free to feed and pet the smaller, tame animals, such as llamas, sheep, pigs, and goats, and it's difficult to determine which enjoys it the most. Adjacent to the zoo on Great Highway is Fleishhacker Playground and a king-sized swimming pool some 1000 by 150 feet in size, holding 6 million gallons of water that is pumped in from the sea.

WHEN THE TIDE is out the beach is a wide stretch of compacted sand where you can walk almost to the base of Cliff House, perched vulnerably between the ocean and Sutro Heights Park. The latter always seems ready to drop onto the highway despite the artificial stone face given it just to prevent such an occurrence. Cliff House, a gift shop, restaurant, and lounge with a fine view of the ocean, has an incendiary history, having burned several times since its erection in 1863. And when the tide comes in even castles may fall to ruin.

GOLDEN GATE BRIDGE – symbol of a city

"THE GOLDEN GATE is one of nature's perfect pictures—let's not disfigure it," began a
notice that appeared in San Francisco newspapers in 1930, campaigning against passage of
a six-county bond issue to finance construction of the Golden Gate Bridge. In the face of
protracted man-made opposition, and in spite of tides, winds, and fogs that led others
to state that it couldn't (or shouldn't) be built, the bridge was constructed and today
stands as a monument to one of the most spectacular engineering accomplishments of all
time. Though no longer the country's longest single suspension bridge, it is still the
most widely recognized symbol of San Francisco. Unique in conception, Golden Gate
Bridge is the result of pioneering in law, finance, engineering, and construction.

SAN FRANCISCO ANCHORAGE was designed by Joseph Strauss, chief bridge construction engineer, to spare Fort Point. Except for the high arch over the fort, anchorage at the bridge's Marin end is the same, consisting of three separately poured, massive concrete blocks (see drawing) keyed into one another by their stair-step configuration. Object of the anchorage is to resist cables' pull due to their own weight as well as to bridge load.

How Golden Gate Bridge is Tied Down

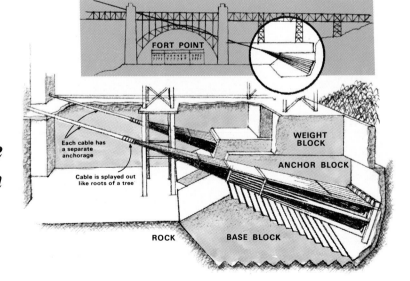

FORT POINT

Each cable has a separate anchorage

Cable is splayed out like roots of a tree

WEIGHT BLOCK

ANCHOR BLOCK

ROCK

BASE BLOCK

HEIGHTS are taken in stride by large crew that keeps up a comprehensive, continuous program of inspection and maintenance. Historic photo at left shows bridge half-completed in 1936 at a time when decks reached out in both directions from the two towers.

IT'S FIVE HUNDRED FEET DOWN to the traffic deck (opposite page), 750 feet down to the water. In the distance is the presidio, and beyond that a slightly tipsy horizon, caused by the photographer keeping a firm grip on his perch atop the north tower.

THE BRIDGE that goes through an island

SAN FRANCISCO-OAKLAND BAY BRIDGE and Golden Gate Bridge were completed in 1936-37, and their opening of the city to the east and the north started the end of the bay's ferry boat era. The Bay Bridge's suspension section and cantilever section (pulled by camera lens into distorted proximity in photo above) are both double-decked to accommodate a constant flow of traffic. At north end of Yerba Buena Island is Treasure Island (out of picture to left), constructed for the Golden Gate International Exposition of 1939-40 and now command center for U.S. Navy activities in the Pacific Theater.

WEST CROSSING OF Bay Bridge is actually two suspension bridges anchored in the center to a massive concrete pier. Drawing below shows how the Yerba Buena tunnel was "built" first and the hole excavated afterward by boring three pilot tunnels, clearing a channel between them (which served as a partial form for pouring the concrete walls), then blasting the core out. This unusual method eliminated the necessity for shoring up during digging and allowed trucks to back right to the face of the core to haul away excavated rock.

The Hole in Yerba Buena Island

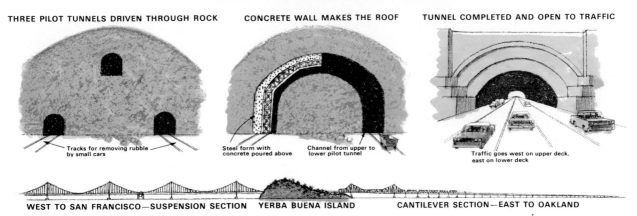

THREE PILOT TUNNELS DRIVEN THROUGH ROCK

Tracks for removing rubble by small cars

CONCRETE WALL MAKES THE ROOF

Steel form with concrete poured above

Channel from upper to lower pilot tunnel

TUNNEL COMPLETED AND OPEN TO TRAFFIC

Traffic goes west on upper deck, east on lower deck

WEST TO SAN FRANCISCO—SUSPENSION SECTION   YERBA BUENA ISLAND   CANTILEVER SECTION—EAST TO OAKLAND

A TUNNEL 150 miles long...full of water

CRYSTAL SPRINGS LAKES (view above is looking south), along with San Andreas Lake, form the storage for San Francisco's water supply. The reservoirs are located in San Mateo County and are situated in the canyons and deep gullies of the San Andreas earthquake fault zone, a natural sink in this area whose valleys have been modified into huge catch basins that trap additional rain water from the surrounding hills.

HETCH HETCHY SUPPLY ROUTE

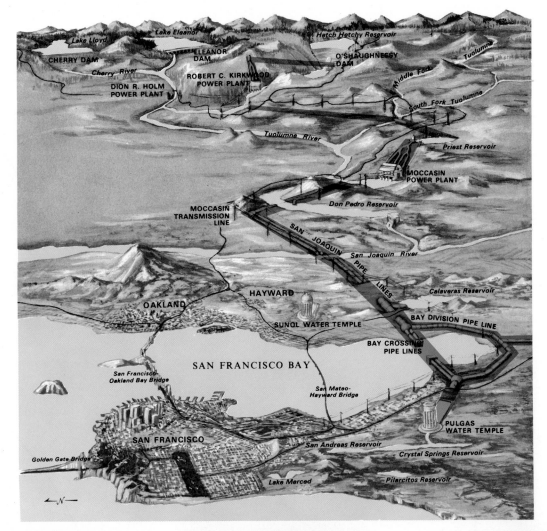

Labels on the map, clockwise: Lake Lloyd, Lake Eleanor, Hetch Hetchy Reservoir, CHERRY DAM, ELEANOR DAM, O'SHAUGHNESSY DAM, Tuolumne, Cherry River, ROBERT C. KIRKWOOD POWER PLANT, Middle Fork, DION R. HOLM POWER PLANT, South Fork Tuolumne, Tuolumne River, Priest Reservoir, MOCCASIN POWER PLANT, MOCCASIN TRANSMISSION LINE, Don Pedro Reservoir, SAN JOAQUIN PIPE LINES, San Joaquin River, Calaveras Reservoir, HAYWARD, OAKLAND, SUNOL WATER TEMPLE, BAY DIVISION PIPE LINE, BAY CROSSING PIPE LINES, SAN FRANCISCO BAY, San Francisco Oakland Bay Bridge, San Mateo-Hayward Bridge, PULGAS WATER TEMPLE, SAN FRANCISCO, San Andreas Reservoir, Crystal Springs Reservoir, Golden Gate Bridge, Lake Merced, Pilarcitos Reservoir

IN EARLY YEARS *water was brought to San Francisco from Marin County on rafts, and throughout the latter half of the 1800's local water sources were exploited by private concerns. After bitter struggles with several monopolistic interests, the City and County of San Francisco began construction of the Hetch Hetchy system, which pipes water all the way from the Tuolumne River in Yosemite National Park. Photos above show construction of new pipeline across San Joaquin Valley; a visible stretch of overhead pipe along Edgewood Road in Redwood City; Pulgas Water Temple, off Canada Road west of San Carlos, where the line empties into Crystal Springs Reservoir.*

THE BIG PARK that has something for everyone

GOLDEN GATE PARK, famed as the kind of park every city should have, is a tribute to the vision of William Hall, first park engineer, and the Scottish tenacity of Superintendent "Uncle" John McLaren, who refused to believe that a three-mile stretch of shifting sand was untamable. The park is entirely man-made and its variety is indeed impressive. The gingerbread flower conservatory—a humid, tropical wonderland—was manufactured in New York and shipped around the Horn in crates. Polo field is one of many game fields in the park; others include baseball diamonds, lawn bowling greens, even a golf course.

STRYBING ARBORETUM—Sunset Magazine *Demonstration Home Gardens* (above) *offer home gardeners a rich variety of ideas for plantings, paving, fencing, patio construction, garden seating, and plant containers. The garden pavilion, designed by Thomas Church and Associates, "floats" over a dry water course. Breathtaking Rhododendron Dell (at left) is another of the park's botanical highlights. Among the cultural attractions are M. H. de Young Museum, California Academy of Sciences, and Spreckels Music Temple.*

JAPANESE TEA GARDEN, opposite page, is perhaps the most peaceful place in the park, even on a week-end, when children clamber over its high-arched moonbridge. The five-tiered pagoda looks down on a quiet pool that reflects old stone lanterns brought from Japan. In the garden there is also a contemplative bronze Buddha and a handsome gift shop. A far cry from the serenity of sipping tea is the vigorous lacrosse game (above) being played on one of the many turfed fields in Golden Gate Park.

THE DYNAMICS OF ENTERPRISE   **249**

With all of its exuberance, San Francisco is deliberate in action, cautious in commitment. Though vitally aware of how its own problems are intertwined with the growing pains of the entire state, the City by the Bay meets the important needs of today while preserving the rich heritage of yesterday.

GROWTH...AND CHANGING NEEDS

Market Street of tomorrow: new brick, trees, benches . . . old lamp posts.

S AN FRANCISCANS are justifiably proud of their city; its attributes are known throughout the world; its historical charms are recognized by residents and visitors alike. But not everything that was good for an earlier day may be good for today. Changes occur . . . some for better, some for worse. Change is inevitable, and though San Franciscans have a profound respect for the city's exciting past, the acceptance of modern times is recognized by all.

A unique and colorful history must indeed be cherished, but a person—or a city—cannot live in the past without becoming isolated from the rest of society. San Franciscans know this. And a growing number of them also know that the need to preserve their city's priceless natural assets has never been more acute. History can lull, but it can also teach—and if its lessons are heeded, San Franciscans will see to it that their hills, their climate, and their bay become the key considerations in future growth and development.

The Old Town Comes Back

THE WHEEL TURNS FULL CIRCLE. San Francisco—as few other cities—is evidence that the past is prologue. Portsmouth Plaza, once the center of town, then a neglected corner of Chinatown and North Beach, is once again becoming an important hub of the city.

In the earliest days, the northeastern end of the city was mostly water; then it was ships at anchor; then it was filled area that extended the city's shoreline. There the Barbary Coast blossomed. There Portsmouth Plaza bloomed as the early center of town. Later, activity moved out to other areas—near the mission, to Nob Hill, to south of Market Street. Today, however, this part of the city is a focal point for new and exciting developments. Jackson Square, site of the old Barbary Coast, has become a delightful place for strollers, and a profitable place for the decorating trade. Nearby, on the site of the city's old produce district, has risen an imposing complex of apartments and business buildings—the Golden Gateway. Adjacent is planned the International Market Place and Embarcadero Center. Even Portsmouth Plaza is slated for great things, what with a Chinese Cultural Center going up across the street.

And every day Market Street is getting closer to what it has always seemed destined for—being the most handsome thoroughfare of the most handsome city.

REFLECTIONS OF YESTERDAY in the windows of today. Telegraph Hill, site of some
of the earliest settlements in old San Francisco, shows dramatically in the façade of the Bank
of America building, whose windows are a modern version of the classic bay window.

PUTTING THE PAST to use is good business

COMMERCIAL ENTERPRISES *that reflect the mood of an earlier day have proven so successful that wise merchants seek out old structures that will have instant appeal to personal nostalgia. Merryvale, Inc.—a retail-wholesale antique salesroom in the 3600 block of Buchanan—is housed comfortably in a brick structure that originally held storage tanks for San Francisco Gas Light Company. The present owners sandblasted the interior to expose the natural brick, left the exterior essentially as it was when the building was constructed in the late 1800's.*

THROUGHOUT THE WEEK, from opening to closing, crowds jam Ghirardelli Square (below) and The Cannery (right). Because of the great variety of shopping offered in centralized and picturesque surroundings that are in keeping with the spirit of the city, such complexes attract more per-day business than their contemporary counterparts.

SOME OF THE BEST SHOPS have nothing for sale. Jackson Square, headquarters for a large number of wholesale decorator showrooms, was once part of the city's colorful Barbary Coast, is now a favorite place for strolling and window shopping. Resurrection of its Gold Rush vintage buildings began around 1953 and continues with the addition of new wholesale and retail outlets, such as One Jackson Place, once a paper warehouse, now a yellow brick compound with a gaslit courtyard providing access to shops, showrooms, and an Irish-pub restaurant.

...PUTTING THE PAST TO USE

Centers of Restored Elegance

Imaginative renovations have been revitalizing some neglected sectors of San Francisco—most notably the old Barbary Coast, the north waterfront, and Cow Hollow—and transforming them into big business areas as well as prime attractions for visitors and residents alike.

This restoration drama began in 1951 when a group of home furnishing wholesalers bought several dilapidated buildings on Jackson Street's 400-block and set about refurbishing them. Today Jackson Square is a tree-shaded stretch that embraces pockets of the past along adjacent alleys and streets and extends through Pacific Avenue's 500-block.

Another crumbling area had been all but forgotten along the north waterfront. For over a century the multi-level red brick mass at the base of Russian Hill belched smoke and steam, first as a woolen works, later as Domingo Ghirardelli's spice and chocolate factory. Then in 1963 William M. Roth spent $14 million creating Ghirardelli Square, an inviting miscellany of shops, galleries, restaurants, and plazas. The same formula of preservation and renovation inspired Leonard V. Martin to remodel the old Del Monte fruit plant, built in 1894, at Fisherman's Wharf nearby. The Cannery, which began operating in 1967, is now a $7.5 million complex with everything under one enormous roof.

Today's merchants are also doing distinctive things where dairy herds once grazed in the heart of Cow Hollow. Along the 1700- to 2200-block of Union Street, they've turned cowbarns, carriage houses, and Victorian dwellings into a fashionable shopping sector with a charming turn-of-the-century flavor.

MARKET STREET comes into its own

THESE DAYS the sun seems to shine with special favor on Market Street and adjoining blocks. Though other parts of the city are undergoing rejuvenation, the downtown area—long in need of a face lifting—appears destined for great things, what with a new subway under the ground and proliferating high-rise above it.

...MARKET STREET

THE NEW IS BUILT on the old, and buildings of today dwarf yesterday's skyscrapers, but the mixture is not at all unpleasing to the eye. For the fourth time in little over a hundred years the city's downtown area is undergoing a major change, a change that offers visionaries a tremendous challenge. In conjunction with the development of a rapid transit system, planners are hard at work beautifying a 3-mile stretch of Market Street, and as always in San Francisco, history has a way of making itself known. During tunneling under Market, and in the driving of pilings for new downtown buildings, traces of several old ships that were sunk and buried in the 1800's have been discovered. Interpretive drawing below shows earth's structure in the vicinity of Market Street and estimated locations of five old vessels whose hulls were covered over by 30 to 50 feet of fill to supply the city's demand for more room.

The Ships that Lie Beneath Market Street

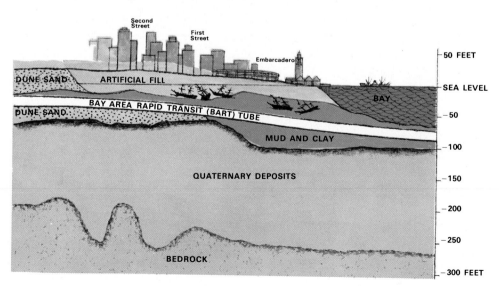

ZELLERBACH PLAZA is a generous, excellently landscaped place that has added a fresh touch to an old thoroughfare. Zellerbach Building, just out of picture to left, was one of the first of contemporary additions to Market Street that gave a new look to the downtown area. The black monolith that rose to an equivalent of twenty stories was at first a startling change to the city's white skyline, but residents soon took pride in a highrise that occupied relatively little airspace.

STANDARD OIL PLAZA is a peaceful garden spot in the busy 300 block of Market Street, a quiet retreat where flowers are constantly in bloom, where shoppers and office workers sit by a sparkling pool during the noon hour. The plaza is a harbinger of other downtown green areas to come.

BART – big link for a network of communities

BAY AREA RAPID TRANSIT system promises a new dimension in regional travel and is expected to have far-reaching effects on San Francisco, since historically, growth follows good transportation. Although many eastern cities have had subways for years, undergrounding in San Francisco was long in coming owing to early qualms regarding earthquake danger. BART is the West's first urban transit system designed specifically to compete with the automobile and hence to reduce congestion from the region's streets and freeways. Some of the system's aims are: 80-mile-an-hour top speeds; 90-second intervals between trains; capacity for 30,000 passengers per hour on each track. Rendering shows three-level routing typical of downtown San Francisco stops. Upper level is passenger mezzanine; middle level accommodates Muni rail lines; lower level carries BART trains.

PASSENGER STATIONS are being individually designed by more than a dozen Bay Area architectural firms to conform with the environment of each community. Clear-span ceilings, sloping walls, and soft, hidden lighting are features of the 16th Street Mission Station shown in model at right. At all stations vending machines provide magnetically coded fare tickets that actuate passenger gates.

AUTOMATIC TRAIN CONTROL CENTER, headquarters for Bay Area Rapid Transit, and the system's Lake Merritt subway station are all contained in a complex between 8th and 9th Avenues in Oakland, shown here in a tabletop model. A landscaped plaza flows under the building and around the subway entrances.

BART CAR is a 70-foot-long vehicle seating 72 passengers. It has carpeted floors, wide aisles, recessed lighting, large tinted windows, and automatic air conditioning that adjusts to all temperature variations in the Bay Area. Even the train track is a special design, its gauge being almost a foot wider than standard for better speed and stability. Tracks are mounted on rubber fasteners to give a smoother and quieter ride.

...LINKING A NETWORK OF COMMUNITIES

BAY AREA RAPID TRANSIT ROUTE

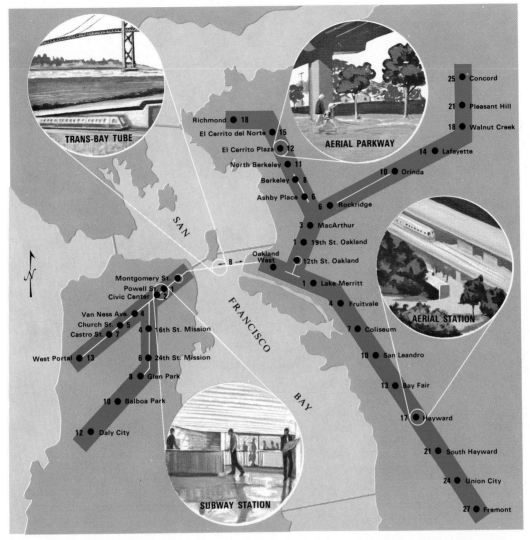

TRANS-BAY TUBE

AERIAL PARKWAY

AERIAL STATION

SUBWAY STATION

SAN FRANCISCO BAY

25 ● Concord
21 ● Pleasant Hill
18 ● Walnut Creek
14 ● Lafayette
10 ● Orinda

Richmond ● 18
El Cerrito del Norte ● 15
El Cerrito Plaza ● 12
North Berkeley ● 11
Berkeley ● 8
Ashby Place ● 6
6 ● Rockridge
3 ● MacArthur
1 ● 19th St. Oakland
← 8 → Oakland West
● 12th St. Oakland
1 ● Lake Merritt
4 ● Fruitvale
7 ● Coliseum
10 ● San Leandro
13 ● Bay Fair
17 ● Hayward
21 ● South Hayward
24 ● Union City
27 ● Fremont

Montgomery St. ●
Powell St. ● 2
Civic Center ●
Van Ness Ave. ● 4
Church St. ● 5
Castro St. ● 7
4 ● 16th St. Mission
6 ● 24th St. Mission
8 ● Glen Park
West Portal ● 13
10 ● Balboa Park
12 ● Daly City

OF THE 75 MILES OF ROUTES extending along BART travel corridors, there are 19 miles of subway lines (indicated above by white station connections), 27 miles of surface lines, 25 miles of aerial lines, and a 4-mile underwater trans-bay tube. The small numbers shown next to main passenger stations indicate minutes required for rush hour travel between San Francisco's Montgomery Street station and San Francisco stops, or between Oakland's 12th Street station and East Bay stops. Suburban stations are equipped with commuter parking areas and transfer facilities for bus passengers. Rail lines are grade-separated to prevent interference by other types of traffic, and provisions are made in their design for future route extensions into other Bay Area cities and counties.

A BOLD PROGRAM of redevelopment
to serve the city

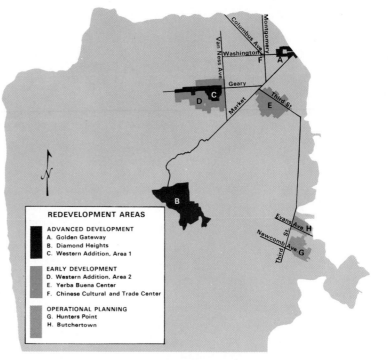

REDEVELOPMENT AREAS

ADVANCED DEVELOPMENT
A. Golden Gateway
B. Diamond Heights
C. Western Addition, Area 1

EARLY DEVELOPMENT
D. Western Addition, Area 2
E. Yerba Buena Center
F. Chinese Cultural and Trade Center

OPERATIONAL PLANNING
G. Hunters Point
H. Butchertown

*SAN FRANCISCO MAYOR Joseph L. Alioto
has emphasized that if San Francisco is not
to go the way of so many other cities it must
intensify its efforts to provide a decent physical
and social environment for its citizens. Thus,
redevelopment is less a matter of architecture and
more a matter of solving economic and sociologic
problems. Early renewal projects were the
target of reproof inasmuch as some critics felt
that blighted areas were turned into attractive
neighborhoods but did not answer the
needs of residents of the former slums. In more
recent years the San Francisco Redevelopment
Agency—working closely with neighborhood
representatives—has made increasing efforts to
provide low-to-moderate income housing.
Endeavor in Western Addition Area 2, aided by
contributions of Black and Japanese-American
leaders, has produced the first step in a long series
of socially oriented housing developments to
come. Peace Pagoda at left is a landmark of
Western Addition's Japanese Cultural and
Trade Center.*

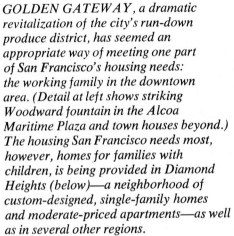

*GOLDEN GATEWAY, a dramatic
revitalization of the city's run-down
produce district, has seemed an
appropriate way of meeting one part
of San Francisco's housing needs:
the working family in the downtown
area. (Detail at left shows striking
Woodward fountain in the Alcoa
Maritime Plaza and town houses beyond.)
The housing San Francisco needs most,
however, homes for families with
children, is being provided in Diamond
Heights (below)—a neighborhood of
custom-designed, single-family homes
and moderate-priced apartments—as well
as in several other regions.*

...REDEVELOPMENT

ONE OF SEVERAL *private developments that promises to give fresh life to a 17-acre sector of the city below the eastern slope of Telegraph Hill is International Market Center, which is to include a home furnishings market, a grand concourse of shops and restaurants, a major hotel. Topping the buildings will be a virtual garden of Babylon—roof-level parks, fountains, outdoor cafes, view areas.*

CHINESE CULTURAL AND TRADE CENTER, *another project of the Redevelopment Agency, located on the site of the Old Hall of Justice, will include a 500-room hotel, a broad, landscaped pedestrian bridge over Kearny Street to connect with Portsmouth Plaza, and a 20,000 square-foot center that will accommodate educational and cultural activities and offer a suitable location for the preservation and exhibition of valuable art treasures from the Orient.*

YERBA BUENA CENTER, above, is only a small part of Redevelopment Agency's plans for refurbishing south of Market. Major objectives of the Center are to overcome the age-old Market Street barrier, to link the area with downtown retail and financial districts, and thus to improve its access and outlook. Plans include office buildings (tallest structure in the model fronts on Market), a sports arena, a convention center, and multi-level garages.
Overall view at right is of the proposed, privately funded Embarcadero Center to rise in downtown San Francisco as a pre-planned addition to the city's present financial district. It features a sky-reaching tower and other office structures, a hotel (right background), an entertainment district, shops, and a pedestrian mall.

TO PROTECT and enhance the Bay

THE BAY WAS HERE before San Francisco, but the challenge of the times is, will it survive San Francisco? Over the years a large portion has been diked off or filled in to provide more usable land, but sometimes the reclamation has been to the detriment of the very people it should have served. Map shows how pattern of extending shoreline around San Francisco alone has developed since 1860 (note correlation between 1906 earthquake damage and filled areas). In 1965 the State-sponsored Bay Conservation and Development Commission set out to explore ways of preserving the bay and practical means of utilizing it without destroying it.

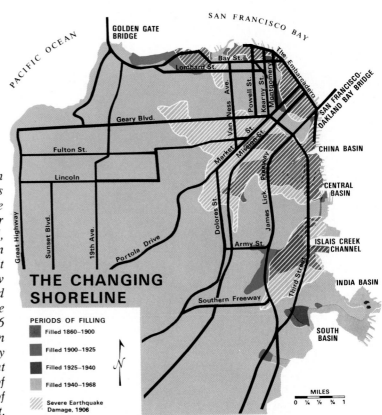

THE CHANGING SHORELINE

PERIODS OF FILLING

Filled 1860–1900

Filled 1900–1925

Filled 1925–1940

Filled 1940–1968

Severe Earthquake Damage, 1906

MILES
0 ¼ ½ ¾ 1

WORKING MODEL of San Francisco Bay, created by the Army Corps of Engineers in Sausalito, is an education for anyone interested in seeing the effects of extensive land fills. The 1/1000 scale model is used in making studies of tides and currents in connection with changes in the bay. When water is run in, the cycle of the tides is created at 15-minute intervals. Portion shown here is San Francisco's North Waterfront, with Municipal Pier curving out near the end of Hyde Street Pier.

HE'S SPIED A SANDPIPER hidden in the marsh. A large part of the value of the bay lies in its potential as a habitat of fish and wildlife. The open water, mudflats, and marshlands form a complex biological system in which living things exist in a delicate balance created by nature. Changes such as filling or dredging may have far-reaching effects on the area's animal life and on its weather.

NEW IDEAS   **271**

SAN FRANCISCO BAY both links and physically divides the area's cities, which form a unique economic community. The bay moderates the concentration of people; it helps to create a natural air conditioning for San Francisco; it provides water-related recreation facilities. To the people who live on its shores, San Francisco Bay is a body of water to be cherished and protected.

Special Supplement

1000 B.C. An early civilization lives on the southern shores of San Francisco Bay. Some 3,000 years later, anthropologist Bert A. Gerow of Stanford University will rate finds unearthed in East Palo Alto as older than 1000 B.C. With them he will find "quantities of red ochre, whole shell beads, stone seedgrinding implements and bone fishhooks." (*San Francisco Chronicle,* November 11, 1968.)

1579 A.D. English freebooter Sir Francis Drake, in his 100-ton vessel, *Golden Hinde,* visits the coast of California near latitude 38° (probably Drake's Bay). "He found a 'faire and good Baye' where he landed, beached, repaired and cleaned his vessels, and built a fort in which he stored his treasure and food supplies. Here he met and had friendly intercourse with the Indians. So pleased was he with this harbor and the territory adjacent to it that he annexed this country to the crown of England under the name Nova Albion." (Robertson, J. W., *Francis Drake Along the Pacific Coast,* Grabhorn Press, San Francisco, 1927.)

1603. Sebastian Vizcaino, Basque explorer, anchors *Capitana* behind a point called La Punta de los Reyes (The Point of the Kings—today's Point Reyes) but does not go ashore.

J. W. Robertson writes: "Of all expeditions sent out by the viceroys this is the most important. Vizcaino not only observed and mapped the entire Pacific Coast as far north as Cape Mendocino, but in many instances names he gave the bays, capes, and islands have been retained. The topographical findings, while not accurate above 38°, gave an excellent general idea of Pacific Coast."

1769. The entrance to San Francisco Bay, La Boca del Puerto (The Mouth of the Port), is discovered on November 1 by Sergeant Jose Ortega, pathfinder of Gaspar de Portola's land expedition, which set out from San Diego in June. The party's diarist, Father Juan Crespi, reports: "This is not an estuary proper, but a large arm of the sea which enters the land for at least 10 leagues [a league is equal to 2½ to 4½ miles]. At narrowest point it must be about three leagues, and at the widest expanse it must be four. In a word, it is a very large and fine harbor, such that not only all the navy of our Most Catholic Majesty but those of all Europe could take shelter in it." (Bolton, Herbert Eugene, *Fray Juan Crespi, Missionary Explorer on the Pacific Coast, 1769-1774,* University of California, Berkeley, 1927, XXXII–XXXIII.)

1774. Captain Don Fernando de Rivera y Moncado, military commander of Alta California, leaves

Monterey and visits the shores of the Golden Gate. Excerpts from his diary (December 4), note: "I set out for the mouth with four soldiers before dinner; we were accompanied by Father Palou. I succeeded in treading the beach, and came to a stand upon the very point on the south side, the one with the three rocks . . . The width of the entrance must be a short quarter-league; it looks westward, and nearly opposite it lies one of the groups of the Farallones." Father Palou places cross on point.

1775. In August Jose Canizares and ten men leave the *San Carlos* in a dugout hollowed from a redwood tree and enter San Francisco Bay in search of anchorage. The log of the *San Carlos* records: "In evening, Don Juan Manuel de Ayala, lieutenant of the frigate of the Royal Navy, ordered anchor dropped off Fort Point . . . . It was thought a good idea to examine another Island, which was found to be very steep and barren and would not afford shelter even for the launch. This island was called 'Alcatraz' [pelican] on account of the abundance of those birds that were on it. Fifteen Indians came on a raft and were taken on board, where they were entertained and given something to eat. They learned how to ask for bread in Spanish." (Robertson, J. W., *Francis Drake Along the Pacific Coast,* Grabhorn Press, San Francisco, 1927.)

1776. Lieutenant Colonel Juan Bautista de Anza, Jose Joaquin Moraga, Father Pedro Font (Spanish leaders of a land expedition from Sonora, Mexico, to Monterey), and some soldiers arrive at Point Lobos, where Father Palou's cross is still standing. Font writes: "Indeed, although in my travels I saw very beautiful sights and beautiful country, I saw none which pleased me so much as this."

Anza plants a cross on a steep bluff overhanging the Golden Gate (at site of present Fort Point) where he proposes to establish a presidio or fort. The expedition pitches camp by Laguna de los Dolores (Lagoon of Sorrows—site of Mission Dolores) and awaits arrival of the Spanish supply ship *San Carlos* from Monterey, thus becoming the first settlers in the Bay Area. On June 29, Father Palou offers the first Mass.

1792. George Vancouver, aboard the British sloop-of-war, *Discovery,* anchors in Yerba Buena cove. "Having passed the inner points of entrance we found ourselves in a very spacious sound, which had the appearance of containing a variety of as excellent harbors as all the known world affords." (Vancouver, George, *A Voyage of Discovery, The North Pacific Ocean and Around the World, Vol. I,* for G. G. and J. Robinson, London, 1798.)

1811. Russians establish a colony at Bodega Bay, 60 miles north of San Francisco, and later one at Ross, 30 miles north of Bodega Bay. "These settlements were founded chiefly in order to supply the Russian-American Fur Company with agricultural supplies, but also as fishing stations for procuring the skins of seals and otters, which animals abounded on the coast." (Soule, Frank, and others, *Annals of San Francisco,* Lewis Osborne, Palo Alto, 1966.)

1822. California ceases to be a province of Spain and becomes a part of the Mexican republic.

1835. Richard Henry Dana, Jr., a seagoing law student, arrives in San Francisco Bay, December 4. On December 25 he writes: "This day was Christmas; and as it rained all day long, and there were no hides to take in, and nothing especial to do, the captain gave us a holiday (the first we had had since Boston), and plum duff for dinner. The Russian brig (anchored in harbor) following the Old Style, had celebrated their Christmas eleven days before; when they had a grand blow-out and (as our men said) drank, in the forecastle, a barrel of gin, ate up a bag of tallow, and made a soup of skin." (Dana, Richard Henry, *Two Years Before the Mast,* P. F. Collier and Son, New York, 1909.)

1846. On July 8, Commander John B. Montgomery anchors the *USS Portsmouth* in Yerba Buena Cove; the following day he goes ashore and raises the American flag over the Custom House, claiming California for the United States.

1847. The pueblo of Yerba Buena is officially named "San Francisco" by ordinance of the alcalde or mayor, Washington A. Bartlett. In January the community sees its first newspaper, the weekly *California Star,* published by Mormon leader Sam Brannan and printed off a press in a grist mill. In May the *Californian* appears.

1848. Gold is discovered at John Sutter's sawmill on the American River, at Coloma, on January 24, by James Marshall. "He picked up the substance. It was heavy, of a peculiar color, and unlike anything he had seen in the stream before . . . 'Boys, by God, I believe I have found a gold mine'." (Stone, Irving, *Men To Match My Mountains: The Story of the Opening of the West,* Doubleday, New York, 1956.) Sam Brannan takes a vial of gold dust to San Francisco in May. "He ran down Montgomery Street, hat in one hand and dust in the other, shouting 'Gold! Gold! Gold from the American River!' . . . His was the shout heard 'round the world." (Dillon, Richard, *Fool's Gold: The Biography of John Sutter,* Coward McMann, Inc., New York, 1967.)

The Mexican War ends and on February 2, California is ceded to the United States through the treaty of Guadalupe Hidalgo.

1849. San Francisco's first commercial bank, the Exchange and Deposits Office, opens on Kearny Street (January 9). Pacific Mail Company's first steamer, *California,* arrives from Panama with 365 passengers from New York. Peter H. Burnett is inaugurated first American constitutional governor of California. San Francisco has first of six terrible fires, which burns ". . . fifty houses, valued at $1,250,000."

1850. San Francisco is incorporated on April 15. California is admitted to the Union September 9, and the news reaches the city October 18 when the *Oregon* steams into the bay firing its signal guns. "When the steamer rounded Clark's Point . . . a universal shout arose from ten thousand voices on the wharves, in the streets, upon the hills, housetops, and the world of shipping in the bay." (Soule, Frank, and others, *Annals of San Francisco,* Lewis Osborne, Palo Alto, 1966.)

Forty vessels sail from Hong Kong to San Francisco, bringing 1,000 Chinese emigrants. By the end of 1851, 25,000 will arrive.

1851. The *Flying Cloud,* a superb clipper ship captained by Josiah Creesy, booms into the Golden Gate and anchors off North Beach, just 89 days and 21 hours out of New York—a record for sailing ships (most took nearly 100 days). "The city went wild as the trim *Flying Cloud* stood up the Bay, every stitch of canvas drawing, a big bone in her teeth, slamming to her historic anchorage. It was half an hour before noon on August 31, 1851. The East was within three months of San Francisco by sail!" (Riesenberg, Jr., Felix, *Golden Gate,* Alfred A. Knopf, Inc., New York, 1940.)

Fires destroy the business district in May and rage through 16 blocks of the city in June. In its four months' existence the first Vigilance Committee of San Francisco hangs four miscreants. "First victim of the vigilantes was John Jenkins, arraigned . . . on charges of stealing a safe . . . and hanged from the veranda of the old City Hotel." (Hanna, Phil Townsend, *California Through Four Centuries,* Holt, Rinehart, New York, 1935.)

1852. Fifteen-foot-deep cisterns are built beneath San Francisco streets to store water; the first is dug, made of tar-drenched plank, at California and Montgomery Streets. They are filled with water hauled in carts from springs nearby. When the 1906 earthquake breaks the city's mains, water from these old underground receptacles will be used to fight the fire.

The Atlantic & Pacific of Wells,

Life of San Francisco

Fargo & Company Express opens an office in Sam Brannan's block between California and Sacramento. Ads placed in the *Alta California* about the company's first eastward shipment July 31 on the steamer *Oregon* announce: "Gold dust, coin and bullion received for shipment until Friday at 4 P.M. Bills of exchange for sale, and gold dust bought at current rates."

1853. California's first telegraph line is stretched from a tower near Point Lobos to a semaphore atop Telegraph Hill.

A branch of the U.S. Mint opens April 3 on Commercial Street. The assayer is Agoston Haraszthy, later famous owner of Sonoma vineyards, and the bookkeeper is Bret Harte, later a well known writer.

1856. Vigilantes reorganize after shooting of James King of William, editor of San Francisco's *Evening Bulletin*. Eighty thousand members turn number 41 Sacramento Street into "Fort Gunnybags" and hang both King's killer (James Casey), and the murderer of U.S. Marshall William H. Richardson (Charles Cora). "A church bell tolled. Every bell in San Francisco answered. As the funeral procession of James King of William left the Unitarian Church a block away, the executioner cut the ropes." (Stone, Irving, *Men To Match My Mountains: The Story of the Opening of the West*, Doubleday, New York, 1956.)

1859. Silver-nitrate ore is discovered on Sun Mountain in the Sierra Nevada, and San Franciscans flock to Nevada with all the enthusiasm of the Gold Rush days. Great profits from the Comstock mines are invested in San Francisco's waning economy, and for the next two decades the city will undergo a business boom.

1860. The Pony Express speeds mail to San Francisco. "Eighty riders, 500 horses—galloping in relays through shriveling sun, through blizzard . . . through Indian banditry . . . riding seventy-five miles a day across the buffalo-trampled plains . . . The rate was $5 a half-ounce." (Dobie, Charles C., *San Francisco A Pageant*, D. Appleton-Century Company, New York, 1935.)

1861. United States Army builds Fort Point to defend the Golden Gate, thus replacing Spanish fortification *El Castillo de San Joaquin*.

After Fort Sumter's surrender in South Carolina, the California Legislature pledges loyalty to the Union, and Leland Stanford, antislavery Republican, is elected governor. "To Leland Stanford . . . is due . . . praise for the attitude of consistent loyalty maintained by the Golden State during the period of the Civil War." (Hunt, R. and N. Sanchez, *Short History of California*, Crowell, New York, 1929.)

1862. The San Francisco Stock and Exchange Board opens. These are the days of "blooded horses and Nob Hill mansions, mistresses and Poodle Dog champagne, and enough left over to buy Italian counts and British lords for their daughters." (O'Brien, Robert, *This Is San Francisco*, Whittlesey House, New York, 1948.)

1868. The University of California is established March 23 by act of state legislature. Both sexes are to receive equal education, and military training is compulsory for the male student.

1869. The symbolic Golden Spike is driven at Promontory Point, Utah, thus linking the Union Pacific and Central Pacific railroads and guaranteeing the fortunes of the four Railroad Kings—Charles Crocker, Mark Hopkins, Leland Stanford, Collis Huntington.

1873. The first cable car, designed by Andrew S. Hallidie, makes its first trip up Clay Street with 90 passengers. "Everything went well until the steep grade above Powell Street was encountered, when the car stopped . . . Hallidie soon found the cause of the trouble . . . ; lime and sawdust . . . were thrown on the cable . . . and the car and its load were safely hauled to the top of the hill." (Kahn, Edgar M., *Cable Car Days in San Francisco*, rev. ed., Stanford University Press, Palo Alto, 1944.)

1875. The Palace Hotel is built at Market and New Montgomery Streets by one of the Bonanza Kings, William Ralston. Its clientele are the rich: "Gentlemen were wearing silk hats and frock coats; ladies were wearing satins and taffetas, and diamonds on every finger of their hands." (Dickson, Samuel, *San Francisco Kaleidoscope*, Stanford University Press, Palo Alto, 1949.)

1878. The American Speaking Telephone Company in San Francisco issues its first list of subscribers on a single sheet.

1887. John McLaren, a landscape gardener from Scotland, takes over as designer of Golden Gate Park. ". . . he planted the sand dunes with lupines and grass and fertilized them with street sweepings." (Conrad, Barnaby, *San Francisco*, Viking Press, New York, 1959.)

1898. The Ferry Building is built and dominates the San Francisco skyline, thus becoming the chief landmark of the city.

1906. Disaster strikes at 5:13 A.M., April 18. First the earthquake, then the fires kill some 200 persons and destroy 497 blocks and 30,000 buildings. "They fled in whatever they could snatch to cover their night clothes. Several of the women wore opera cloaks, for Caruso had sung the night before. One of the many stories of the earthquake-and-fire was that Caruso ran out of the Palace Hotel shouting, 'Give me my old Vesuvius'." (Atherton, Gertrude, *Golden Gate Country*, Duell, New York, 1945.)

On April 26 the *San Francisco Chronicle* reports: "City lights to gleam tonight; stores open, prices low." The next day its "Best News" briefs include: "Work begins on rebuilding city on new lines; plans for wider streets and parks. All main sewers in good working order. Telegrams from Eastern financial centers report millions ready to be poured into city. Derricks, donkey engines and wrecking crews are already clearing away the debris, yet almost too hot to handle, preparatory to rebuilding."

Lawrence W. Harris expresses mood of most San Franciscans in a cheerful poem circulated on a printed card. It runs, in part:

Put me somewhere east of East
  Street where there's nothing
  left but dust,
Where the lads are all a hustlin'
  and where everything's gone
  bust,
Where the buildin's that are
  standin' sort of blink and
  blindly stare
At the damndest finest ruins ever
  gazed on anywhere."

1915. The Panama-Pacific International Exposition runs from February 20 to December 4, celebrating completion of the Panama Canal. The Palace of Fine Arts, which will become a San Francisco landmark, is the highlight of the exposition. "'Temple' is the proper adjective to use in connection with it—'palace' is far too trite and flamboyant." (Dobie, Charles C., *San Francisco A Pageant*, D. Appleton-Century Company, New York, 1935.)

1917. The infamous Barbary Coast is finally closed by state and city law.

1935. The inaugural trans-Pacific mail flight of the Pan American China Clipper leaves San Francisco Bay for Hawaii and Manila on November 22.

1936. The first passenger trans-Pacific flight of the China Clipper leaves San Francisco on October 21 with seven passengers.

San Francisco-Oakland Bay Bridge opens with gala ceremonies on November 15.

1937. Golden Gate Bridge opens, and festivities last from May 27 to June 13. ". . . Poppies had been sown on both approaches to the bridge, and they blazed their golden welcome. . . . Thousands dashed over, some skating and some on stilts, others wheeling babies." (Older, Cora, *San Francisco: Magic City*, David McKay Company, Inc., New York, 1961.)

1939. On February 19 the Golden Gate International Exposition opens on a 400-acre man-made island (Treasure Island) next to Yerba Buena Island. The fair, commemorating the completion of the two bridges, emphasizes the city's cultural and commercial relations with the Orient and the Pacific. When the exposition closes, plans call for converting this island into an airport.

1941. The Japanese bomb Pearl Harbor, December 7 at 10:05 A.M. San Francisco time and the Pacific Coast springs to wartime alert. California Attorney General Earl Warren, from his office in San Francisco, warns all law enforcement agencies and civilians to guard against disorder and urges that reason and calm prevail. San Francisco Mayor Angelo Rossi calls Defense Council into action. The Golden Gate and San Francisco-Oakland Bay Bridges are put under 24-hour guard, and the Alameda tube is closed. During blackouts, San Franciscans gather on hilltops to watch for enemy planes.

1945. On August 14 Japan surrenders unconditionally at 4 P.M., San Francisco time. The *San Francisco Chronicle's* headline: "City Goes Wild—And Nobody Cares—Every Whistle Summons Crowds—But The Church Bells Ring Too." Its following news report by Charles Raudebaugh says: "Market Street was the center of celebration, but there was hilarity, and excitement and gratitude—and church bells. Air raid sirens sounded first, then auto horns, factory whistles, and ships' whistles—and church bells. Traffic was hopelessly tied up, scarcely a street car could move on Market—all that mattered was the war had ended—and the days of 'blood, sweat and tears' were over."

The United Nations Conference of International Organization at San Francisco is attended by delegates from 50 nations, who sign the United Nations Charter on June 26.

1951. On September 8 the Japanese Peace Treaty is signed at San Francisco by 49 nations, excluding the Soviet Union.

1960's. San Francisco meets the future:

Construction begins on 75-mile Bay Area Rapid Transit System.

The city spruces up some landmarks through commercial development of an old chocolate factory and a former cannery.

Redevelopment is initiated to create better neighborhoods and a greater San Francisco. The initial programs are: the Western Addition, Diamond Heights, the Golden Gateway, the Chinese Cultural Center, Hunter's Point, and the Yerba Buena Center. Other projects in the planning stages are the refurbishing of Market Street and the International Market Place.

Many of San Francisco's place names recall the city's early and colorful heritage. Some names (Potrero Hill, Anza Street, Mission Dolores) date back to the Spanish explorers and settlers, while others (Leidesdorff Street, Geary Street, Larkin Street) refer to the early American days. Some of San Francisco's personalities are also honored, such as Lillie Hitchcock Coit and Samuel Brannan. A few names have undergone several changes—Twin Peaks was once known as Los Pechos de la Choca, Grant Avenue was once Dupont Street, and Maiden Lane was once called Morton Street. There are different schools of thought as to how some names were acquired; in those instances both interpretations are included.

The following material covers San Francisco's best known streets, hills, districts, and areas.

ALCATRAZ ISLAND. This 12-acre island of solid rock lies out in San Francisco Bay 1½ miles north of Fisherman's Wharf. Alcatraz, or "The Rock," gained national fame after it became a federal penitentiary (1934) and housed such notorious gangsters as Al Capone and "Machine Gun" Kelly. Juan Manuel de Ayala discovered the island in 1775 and named it Isla de los Alcatraces or Isle of the Pelicans because of the flocks of pelicans nesting there. (Some say Ayala originally applied this name to Yerba Buena Island; however, the name was incorrectly transferred to "The Rock" in 1826 by a map-maker.) Alcatraz's penal history goes back to 1859 when it was first used as a disciplinary barracks by the U.S. Army, and later as a military prison. In 1963 all the federal prisoners were removed from Alcatraz and its use as a prison was brought to an end.

ANGEL ISLAND. Juan Manuel de Ayala sailed through the Golden Gate on the *San Carlos* in 1775 and anchored off an island he called La Isla de Nuestra Senora de los Angeles or The Island of Our Lady of the Angels. The triangular-shaped island, the largest in San Francisco Bay, is about a mile square. After California joined the Union, Angel Island was used mostly for military purposes. In 1892 it was set up as a quarantine station and remained as such until the 1960's when it became a state park.

ANZA STREET, which traverses the Richmond District from Masonic Avenue to 48th Avenue, was named for Juan Bautista de Anza. It was Anza who led settlers from Mexico to Monterey in 1775, and who in 1776 selected the site for Mission Dolores and established the presidio as a military garrison for the soldiers of Charles II of Spain.

ARGUELLO BOULEVARD, which runs north from Fulton Street to Moraga Avenue in the presidio, bears the name of the Arguello family.

Jose Arguello was head officer of the presidio from 1787 to 1806, and his son, Luis Antonio, was Alta California's first governor.

BRANNAN STREET, which runs parallel to Market Street from the Embarcadero to Tenth Street, was named for Samuel Brannan, a Mormon Elder who arrived at Yerba Buena in 1846 with settlers, a printing press, flour mill machinery, and some farm tools. Brannan was an early-day Jack-of-all-trades. His list of credits in San Francisco include: performing the first marriage and preaching the first sermon under American rule; establishing the city's first newspaper; announcing at Portsmouth Plaza the discovery of gold at Sutter's Mill; and organizing and presiding over the Vigilance Committee.

BRODERICK STREET, which runs unpretentiously north-south from Jefferson Street to Waller Street, was named in behalf of U.S. Senator David C. Broderick. Broderick is best remembered as the loser of the duel with David S. Terry, California Supreme Court Chief Justice, early in the morning of September 13, 1859, near Lake Merced.

COIT TOWER. This fluted cylindrical column, sometimes referred to as a fire-hose nozzle, was built in 1933 with funds left to the city by society matron and fire enthusiast Lillie Hitchcock Coit. At the age of ten, Lillie began chasing the fire wagons, and in 1863 the Knickerbocker Engine Company #5 made her an honorary member. All her life, Lillie attended the annual firemen's banquet, wore a diamond studded gold badge the firemen gave her, and signed her name Lillie Hitchcock Coit—5. Inside the tower, which rises 210 feet from the summit of Telegraph Hill, are murals done by San Francisco artists in 1934 under the Work Projects Administration. An elevator runs to the top of Coit Tower for an exceptionally lofty view of the city and the bay.

COW HOLLOW lies between Vallejo and Greenwich, Lyon and Webster. During the 1860's a man named George Hatman began a dairy ranch on several acres of what is now Union Street, and by the time the Board of Health (1880's) had ordered the cattle to be moved to less-populated areas, San Franciscans had labeled this area Cow Hollow. Today Cow Hollow, with its art galleries, antique shops, and fashionable dwellings, shows no sign of when slaughterhouses, gashouses, the Seaside Gardens, and Herman's Harbor View Park fronted the dunes.

EMBARCADERO, Spanish for pier or wharf, is the name given to the roadway and area which runs along the waterfront from Fisherman's Wharf south to China Basin. Along the Embarcadero are docks which service passenger liners as well as cargo ships. Perhaps the Embarcadero's most famous landmark is the Ferry Building, which has been a welcoming sight to ships entering the port of San Francisco since 1898.

GEARY STREET, one of San Francisco's main thoroughfares running east and west from Market Street to the ocean, was named in honor of Colonel John W. Geary, first mayor of San Francisco. A native of Pennsylvania, Geary was appointed Postmaster of San Francisco by President Polk in 1849 in return for services rendered in the Mexican War. That same year Geary was unanimously elected First Alcalde of San Francisco, and when the city's first charter was adopted in 1850 he became Mayor. In 1852 Geary, not quite 35 years old, refused to run for reelection as mayor, and after just four years in San Francisco he returned to his native Pennsylvania.

GOLDEN GATE. Bobbing around in a small boat off Fort Point, John C. Fremont received his inspiration and first coined the phrase "Golden Gate." It was first put down in writing in his *Geographical Memoir of California* published in 1848—"To this Gate I gave the name of 'Chrysophlae' or Golden Gate, for the same reason the harbor of Byzantium was called 'Chrysoceras,' or Golden Horn." Apparently Fremont was proud to be the originator of a name which had such ready acceptance, for in his *Memoirs of My Life* published in 1886, he wrote "I named it GOLDEN GATE."

Name Come From?

GRANT AVENUE, famous for being the main street of Chinatown, was Yerba Buena's first official street. Francisco de Haro, first alcalde of Yerba Buena, labeled it Calle de la Fundacion (Street of the Founding) in 1834, and one year later William Richardson became its first resident, pitching a tent where 827 Grant is today. With American rule coming to California, it seemed appropriate to change the name, and Alcalde Bartlett selected Dupont, in honor of his friend, Navy Captain Samuel F. Du Pont. After the 1906 earthquake, the name of the entire street was changed to Grant Avenue, after former president Ulysses S. Grant.

JAMES LICK FREEWAY was named for an eccentric Pennsylvanian who worked his way to San Francisco via South America selling pianos. Landing at the bayside village in 1847 with $30,000, Lick, intent on accumulating more of a fortune, invested heavily in what was considered worthless real estate. Among his first ventures were a flour mill in the San Jose area, a fruit orchard in the Santa Clara Valley, and construction of the Lick House, a famous hotel and restaurant of its day. A miser when caring for himself, Lick was a great philanthropist and perhaps his most notable deeds were donation of land and funds for the Lick Observatory atop Mount Hamilton, and donation of funds for the California School of Mechanical Arts, now Lick Wilmerding School.

KEARNY STREET, which runs north and south from Telegraph Hill to Market Street, was named for General Stephen W. Kearny, military governor of California in 1847. During the 1850's, because it bordered Portsmouth Plaza, Kearny was one of San Francisco's busiest streets.

LAGUNA STREET was named after Washerwomen's Lagoon, largest of all the ponds which collected in front of San Francisco's sand dunes. Many women in the mid-1800's carried their laundry to this spot for its weekly wash. Washerwomen's Lagoon, abandoned and filled in when sewage from a tannery on the waterfront polluted the area, was approximately where Filbert and Franklin cross today; Laguna Street lies three blocks west of this intersection.

LARKIN STREET, which runs north-south from Aquatic Park to Market Street, bears the name of Thomas O. Larkin, first and last U.S. Consul for California and an avid worker for the United States cause in California. A native of Massachusetts, Larkin arrived in Monterey in 1832 (his original house still stands there) and worked as a merchant before his involvement in government work. After California joined the Union, the Larkins settled in San Francisco.

LAUREL HILL (California and Presidio). In 1854 Gold Rush settlers established a cemetery on the slopes of a 54-acre hill covered largely with laurel trees. Laurel Hill Cemetery became the final resting place for such famous San Franciscans as James Fair, William Sharon, Mayor James Van Ness, Andrew Hallidie, and Senator David Broderick. In 1937, city officials, feeling the population pressures, ordered all the coffins relocated to peninsula cemeteries to make way for residential and commercial developments.

LEIDESDORFF STREET, an alley off California Street which runs parallel to Montgomery Street, bears the name of William A. Leidesdorff. A native of the Dutch West Indies, he migrated as a boy to New Orleans, became associated with a wealthy cotton merchant, and upon the merchant's death inherited a fortune. A tragic love affair forced Leidesdorff to leave the South, and he wandered on the high seas until finally landing in San Francisco in 1841. Here he took an active part in civic affairs— he participated with Fremont in the Sonoma Bear Flag Revolt, acted as American vice-consul for Yerba Buena, and was its first elected American alcalde. Leidesdorff is buried at Mission Dolores.

MAIDEN LANE (between Union Square and Kearny Street). In the rollicking tradition of the Barbary Coast, this narrow two-block alley, then called Morton Street, was known for its bawdiness and corruption. The 1906 fire left Morton Street in ruins, and hoping for a more reputable future, city officials renamed the street Union Square Avenue, which was changed in 1921 to Manila Avenue. By 1922 independent businesses had begun to front both sides of the alley and a Kearny Street jeweler suggested another name change—Maiden Lane—in honor of New York's jewelry and silverware trade center.

MARINA (between the Bay and Lombard Street, Fort Mason and the Presidio). The area referred to as the Marina was once a cove and was filled in to house the Panama-Pacific International Exposition of 1915. When the fair closed, all the buildings except the Palace of Fine Arts were torn down, and half the waterfront became a yacht harbor or marina, and the other half a park, called the Marina Green. The Marina was slow in developing, but in the late 1920's and 1930's, builders began constructing solid rows of tile-roofed homes and small apartments. Today the Marina is a favorite spot for Sunday sun bathers and boat watchers.

MCLAREN RIDGE bears the name of John McLaren, Scottish gardener and superintendent of Golden Gate Park from 1887 to 1943. Located in the southeast section of San Francisco, McLaren Ridge comprises several hundred acres, most of which are being developed into John McLaren Park for public use.

...Where Did that Name Come From?

MISSION DISTRICT, which lies south of Market Street and begins where Mission Street changes direction and heads south, takes its name from San Francisco's Mission Dolores. Mission Street, the district's main thoroughfare, follows the old trail which linked Yerba Buena Village with the mission. This district is noted for its excellent weather and its large segments of Irish and Spanish-speaking residents.

MISSION DOLORES (Dolores and 16th Street). Lieutenant Colonel Juan Bautista de Anza selected a site for a mission in honor of St. Francis alongside a stream which he called Arroyo de los Dolores because it was the feast day of Our Lady of Sorrows. The name Dolores soon became attached to the nearby lake (long since filled) and eventually to the mission.

MONTGOMERY STREET, San Francisco's financial district and "Wall Street of the West," bears the name of Captain John B. Montgomery, who landed the *USS Portsmouth* in 1846 approximately at Clay and Montgomery Streets and raised the American flag over the Custom House at Yerba Buena's plaza.

MOUNT DAVIDSON (between Portola Drive and Monterey Boulevard). The highest point in San Francisco, at 938 feet, Mount Davidson is covered with eucalyptus and pines planted by Adolph Sutro and the city's school children in the 1880's. George Davidson, a government surveyor, surveyed the peak in 1852 and named it Blue Mountain. In 1911 it was renamed in his honor. Mount Davidson is usually deserted except at Easter when worshippers climb to the summit (there are no roads, only trails) for annual sunrise services held under the 103-foot concrete cross.

MOUNT OLYMPUS (17th and Clayton). Mount Olympus stands directly in the center of San Francisco, and from its summit (a city park with an elevation of 570 feet) there is an impressive view in all directions. A local yarn says this relatively unknown hill was named for "Old Limpus" Hanrahan, a crippled neighborhood milk peddler; others say it was named Mount Olympus because its view was fit for the gods.

NOB HILL. In 1856 a Dr. Arthur Hayne cut a trail through the thick brush to the top of Nob Hill and built, of wood and clay, the first known residence on this hill. In the late 1860's and 1870's the silver and railroad kings followed his example, and each, trying to outdo the other, constructed a magnificent home. The local people referred to these *nouveaux riche* as "nabobs" (men of great wealth or prominence), which is believed to have evolved into Nob. The only mansion to survive the 1906 fire was James Flood's brownstone which today houses the Pacific Union Club.

NORTH BEACH. Although North Beach contains a mixture of nationalities, it is primarily the center of San Francisco's Italian community and a haven for bohemians and artists. Also the hub of the city's night life,

North Beach offers good restaurants, coffee houses, and lively and offbeat night spots. The area was so named in the 1850's when the shore of San Francisco Bay extended far inland between Russian Hill and Telegraph Hill with "North Beach" the protected inlet between.

O'FARRELL STREET was named in behalf of Jasper O'Farrell, an Irishman who came to Yerba Buena in 1843 from Philadelphia. A civil engineer, O'Farrell was chosen in 1847 to revise the street survey made by Jean Jacques Vioget some eight years earlier. O'Farrell corrected Vioget's street angles, which were $2\frac{1}{2}$ degrees off right angles, extended the city's streets in all directions, and laid out Market Street (which he named after a major street in Philadelphia) to parallel the old trail heading from Yerba Buena Cove to the mission.

PORTOLA DRIVE, which connects Upper Market with Junipero Serra Boulevard, was named for Gaspar de Portola, Spanish explorer and leader of the 1769 expedition which discovered San Francisco Bay. Originally seeking Monterey Bay, Portola discovered he had proceeded too far north and dispatched his scout, Sergeant Jose Francisco de Ortega, to find his way to Point Reyes. Ortega (after whom Ortega Street in the Sunset District is named) returned with news of a huge body of water which extended inland north and south. Portola himself viewed the bay from Sweeney Ridge, which lies just above Half Moon Bay.

PORTSMOUTH PLAZA, on Kearny Street between Clay and Washington Streets, was the center of activity for the thirty-some residents of the sleepy village of Yerba Buena during Spanish days. It was here that Captain John Montgomery, after disembarking from the *USS Portsmouth* (which gave the plaza its formal name), raised the American flag over San Francisco for the first time. Although Portsmouth Plaza was the scene of some of early San Francisco's most exciting events, it began to lessen in importance in the 1880's as the city expanded west and south. The park, however, remained much the same until 1960 when it was uprooted to install an underground garage, and then redone in a more modern fashion.

POTRERO HILL (between the James Lick Freeway and Third Street, Army and 16th Street). Old frame houses dot the top of this hill which once served as potrero (Spanish for pasture) for the cattle of Mission Dolores. Sparsely settled first by some Scottish boat builders and then by Russian fugitives in the early 1900's, Potrero Hill today, although its population is varied, retains much of the old Russian flavor: bilingual church signs, elderly women in babushkas or headshawls, elderly gentlemen speaking their native tongue.

RED ROCK HILL. One of three hills which comprise Diamond Heights, Red Rock Hill was relatively untouched until the early 1960's when the land was cleared, streets cut, and homes and apartment buildings constructed. After World War II this 689-foot rock hill which glistened "red in the proper light" was designated as part of a redevelopment area by San Francisco's Board of Supervisors. Until that time, Red Rock Hill had been used solely for quarrying and cattle grazing.

RINCON HILL (between Spear and Second Streets, Folsom and Brannan; south of Market). Early settlers referred to the southern tip of the Yerba Buena Cove as Rincon (Spanish for corner) Point, and the hill rising from its base as Rincon Hill. The most fashionable residential area in the city during the 1850's and 1860's, the neighborhood today is industrial and the hill, much cut away, is hidden under the approaches to the San Francisco-Oakland Bay Bridge.

RUSSIAN HILL (between North Beach and Pacific Heights). Small, little-known parks, steep winding paths, quaint old cottages, skyscraper apartment buildings, and sweeping views make up Russian Hill. No one knows how the hill really acquired its name, but the most accepted version deals with the crest of Vallejo Street being used as burial grounds for Russian sailors. It was the American children in the mid-1800's playing among the graves that began to refer to the hill as "Russian."

SUTRO HEIGHTS (48th and Point Lobos Avenues). On this hill overlooking the ocean Adolph Sutro in the 1880's built a Victorian mansion and developed formal gardens which were opened daily to strollers. A Prussian immigrant, Sutro made his fortune on the Nevada Comstock Lode in the late 1800's, then retired to San Francisco where he built Sutro Baths, rebuilt the Cliff House after it burned the first time, and also served as mayor (1895–97). Now a public park with decaying statues and weathered cypresses recalling the past (the house no longer stands), Sutro Heights gives a commanding view of Ocean Beach to the south and Point Lobos and Land's End to the north.

SUTTER STREET, which runs east-west from Market to Presidio Avenue, was named for John A. Sutter, on whose Coloma land gold was discovered in January of 1848. A Swiss immigrant, Sutter had arrived in Monterey ten years earlier and established a colony of settlers where the American River joined the Sacramento River. Although Sutter's business opportunities were great (purchase of Fort Ross in 1841, Gold Rush, founding of Sacramento), he was a poor businessman and by 1852 had lost all his land and prestige. He left California a bankrupt and broken man and lived in Pennsylvania until his death.

TELEGRAPH HILL (Lombard at Kearny). The early Spaniards referred to this hill as Loma Alta or tall small hill. In the 1840's it was called Windmill Hill, and then Signal Hill when a semaphore was installed to signal the townspeople when ships entered the Golden Gate. In 1853 it became the first Western telegraph station and was officially named Telegraph Hill. Goats were the main occupants of the hill until the turn of the century when the Irish, the Italians, and then the painters, writers, and poets came to claim the hill as theirs. Today a variety of homes, old flats, and tall apartments grace the slopes of the hill.

TENDERLOIN DISTRICT roughly covers the area from Mason to Jones Streets around Eddy and Turk Streets. Defined by the dictionary as a district of a city largely devoted to vice and other forms of law breaking , the term used to apply to Powell Street (close to Market) where lively entertainment rivaled that of the Barbary Coast. As Powell Street began to take on a more respectable atmosphere, the Tenderloin moved just west where not-so-respectable entertainment can still be found. However, the area also contains some fine hotels and a number of outstanding restaurants.

TWIN PEAKS. Indian legend says that Twin Peaks was originally one mountain (man and wife) which was split into two by the Great Spirit with a bolt of lightning because the couple was so quarrelsome. When the Spanish came to Yerba Buena they referred to the peaks as Los Pechos de la Choca (the Breasts of the Indian Maiden) in honor of the lovely daughter of a local chief. These identical or "Twin Peaks" stand almost directly in the center of town, and while their slopes have suc-

cumbed to real estate developments, the summits are public property and have remained relatively untouched. A figure-of-eight road winds around the peaks and from a lookout point San Franciscans can see perhaps the most encompassing view of their city.

UNION SQUARE—a 2.6-acre block bordered by Geary, Powell, Post, and Stockton Streets—is a public park with a four-level underground garage. Presented to the city in 1850 by Mayor Geary, Union Square took its name in 1860 from the pro-Union meetings held there. In 1903 a 97-foot monument commemorating Dewey's victory at Manila Bay was dedicated by President Theodore Roosevelt. During the aftermath of the 1906 earthquake and fire, the Square was used as a place of refuge, mostly for the residents of the St. Francis Hotel. Today Union Square is a haven for all kinds of San Franciscans, who fight for space with the pigeons. Public rallies, scheduled and impromptu, are often held there; annual affairs include Rhododendron Week and the Cable Car Bell Ringing Contest.

VAN NESS AVENUE, named for James Van Ness, mayor elect of San Francisco in 1855, is a main thoroughfare running north and south from Bay Street into the Central Freeway (South Van Ness continues on to Army Street). Once the hub of the German population, Van Ness today is lined with automobile showrooms, churches, motels, hotels, and a variety of restaurants.

WESTERN ADDITION. In the 1860's Van Ness Avenue was the western boundary of San Francisco; when an addition went up west of town, it became known as the Western Addition. This section, which roughly includes the area between Van Ness and Presidio Avenue, Fulton and Broadway, escaped the 1906 fire. During the 1870's and 1880's, Victorian homes with a variety of architectural façades were constructed. Many of those homes, which had deteriorated badly, have been cleared away as part of San Francisco's redevelopment program. Some, however, on the outskirts of the Addition, have been tastefully preserved in the Victorian tradition.

VALLEJO STREET, which runs east-west from the Embarcadero to Lyon Street, bears the name of Mariano de Guadalupe Vallejo, Mexican commandante of the San Francisco presidio. Born and educated in Monterey, Vallejo remained in San Francisco until 1835 when he was instructed to establish the pueblo of Sonoma as a frontier post. When the United States flag flew over Sonoma, Vallejo adjusted to American rule and became one of the town's leading citizens, a delegate to the convention that framed California's first constitution at Monterey in 1849, and a senator in the state's first legislature.

YERBA BUENA. The tiny Spanish village by the huge bay was originally called Yerba Buena (Spanish for good herb) because of the abundance of wild mint growing in the underbrush and over the sand dunes. The name of the town was changed to San Francisco in 1847 by proclamation of the first alcalde of San Francisco under American rule, Lieutenant Washington Bartlett. As published in the *California Star*: "It is Hereby Ordained that the name of San Francisco shall hereafter be used in all official communications and public documents or records appertaining to the town of (Yerba Buena)." Probable reasons for the name change: Larkin and Semple were planning to name a town on the Carquinez Straits 'Francisca'; to prevent confusion with the island and cove named Yerba Buena; San Francisco was a more sophisticated name.

YERBA BUENA ISLAND lies in San Francisco Bay and is anchorage for the two spans of the San Francisco-Oakland Bay Bridge. Frederick W. Beechey, when surveying San Francisco Bay in 1826, named the island Yerba Buena after the wild mint growing there. Later, goats pastured on the hills and the colloquial name became Goat Island. That was the official name which the U.S. Geographic Board decided on in 1896; however, due to an effective campaign, the Board changed the name in 1931 to Yerba Buena. The Island was acquired by the Federal Government in 1866 and today, along with Treasure Island, it services the United States Navy and Coast Guard.

The history of the nine San Francisco Bay Area counties dates back to the late 1700's when Spaniards were exploring the shores, hills, and valleys. Accurate diaries were kept on these expeditions, and today, especially in San Mateo County, there are numerous landmarks designating camping sites of Portola and Anza. As the Spanish began to settle the area, large land grants were given, locations of which are still known today. As the Bay Area came alive with post-gold rush settlers, San Francisco prospered and outlying towns were established. Many buildings, or sites of buildings from that period and on, have been preserved.

The following listing covers selected principal landmarks in the nine counties surrounding San Francisco Bay. All are registered with the California Historical Landmarks Advisory Committee in Sacramento, California. Usually a tablet or plaque marks the site.

SAN FRANCISCO COUNTY

ANCHORAGE OF THE SAN CARLOS IN SAN FRANCISCO BAY. Fort Point, under south end of Golden Gate Bridge. The *San Carlos*, first ship to enter San Francisco Bay, initially dropped anchor just inside the Golden Gate in 1775. In 1794, Castillo de San Joaquin, the harbor's first fortification, was completed, and it lasted until 1853 when the United States Army cut away the cliff and constructed Fort Point. This fort is a partial replica of Fort Sumter, and is the only brick fort west of the Mississippi. Its sea wall has stood undamaged for over 100 years.

PRESIDIO OF SAN FRANCISCO. Arguello Boulevard to Moraga Avenue. A military garrison settled by Lieutenant Jose Moraga for Spain in 1776, the Presidio originally consisted of a square (containing homes, store, church) surrounded by a wall 12 to 15 feet high. Since 1846 the Presidio has been used as an army post on the Pacific Coast. The only original building remaining is used today as the Officers' Club.

SARCOPHAGUS OF THOMAS STARR KING. Franklin and Geary. In the churchyard of the First Unitarian Church is Thomas Starr King's sarcophagus—a white marble tomb. King, a Unitarian minister, is credited with swaying California to join the Union cause during the Civil War.

SITE OF FIRST JEWISH RELIGIOUS SERVICES IN SAN FRANCISCO. Number 4 Columbus. In a second-floor room in a store on this site, forty members of the Jewish faith gathered on Yom Kippur September 26, 1849, to participate in the first Jewish services in San Francisco.

TELEGRAPH HILL. Telegraph Hill. Originally used as a signal station in 1850, Telegraph Hill sported a tall pole with moveable arms which signaled the townspeople as to the type of vessel entering the Golden Gate. In 1853 the first telegraph in California connected Telegraph Hill with Point Lobos, eight miles away.

LANDING PLACE OF CAPTAIN J. B. MONTGOMERY. Southeast corner Montgomery and Clay. On July 9, 1846, in "the days when the water came up to Montgomery Street," Commander John B. Montgomery landed near here on the *USS Portsmouth* and raised the stars and stripes on what is now Portsmouth Plaza.

SITE OF FIRST PUBLIC SCHOOL. Clay and Brenham. A plaque marks the site of the first public school in California. It was opened April 3, 1848, on the southwest corner of Portsmouth Plaza.

SITE OF EASTERN TERMINUS OF CLAY STREET HILL RAILROAD. Clay and Kearny. The Clay Street Hill Railroad, invented and installed by Andrew S. Hallidie, was the first cable railroad system in the world. It began operation August 2, 1873, and lasted until February 15, 1942.

SITE OF MONTGOMERY BLOCK. Southeast corner Montgomery and Washington. A large building constructed here in 1853 was headquarters for many outstanding lawyers, financiers, writers, actors, and artists. James King of William, editor of the *Bulletin*, died here after being shot by James Casey on May 14, 1856. The building was demolished in 1959.

SITE OF FIRST MEETING OF FREEMASONS HELD IN CALIFORNIA. 726 Montgomery Street. In 1849 a charter was granted by the Grand Lodge of the District of Columbia for the organization of California Lodge No. 13, Free and Accepted Masons, now California Lodge No. 1. In November of that year, the Lodge was formally organized under the charter.

PORTSMOUTH PLAZA. Kearny between Clay and Washington. Named for the *USS Portsmouth*, it was in this plaza that Captain J. B. Montgomery raised the American Flag on July 9, 1846.

OLD ST. MARY'S CHURCH. California and Grant. The first building erected as a cathedral in California, Old St. Mary's served the Archdiocese of San Francisco in that capacity from 1854 to 1891. Once the city's most prominent building, much of its stonework was quarried and cut in China, and its brick was brought around Cape Horn.

SITE OF THE WHAT CHEER HOUSE. Southeast corner of Sacramento and Leidesdorff. This is the site of the famous What Cheer House, a unique hotel opened in 1852 by R. B. Woodward and destroyed by the 1906 fire. The What Cheer House catered to men only, permitted no liquor on the premises, and housed San Francisco's first free library and first museum.

UNION SQUARE. Post, Geary, Stockton, and Powell. This square,

deeded for public use January 3, 1850, during the administration of John White Geary, first mayor and postmaster of San Francisco, was the city's center during the middle 1800's. The name originated in 1860 when public meetings in support of the Union were held here.

SITE OF THE MARK HOPKINS INSTITUTE OF ART. California and Mason. In February, 1893, Edward F. Searles donated the Mark Hopkins Mansion to the University of California in trust for the San Francisco Art Institute for "instruction in and illustration of the fine arts, music, and literature," and as San Francisco's first cultural center.

SITE OF OFFICE OF THE STAR. Washington and Brenham. The *California Star*, San Francisco's first newspaper, was published on this site January 9, 1847, by Samuel Brannan with Elbert P. Jones as editor. The paper was later known as *The Alta Californian*.

LONG WHARF. Commercial, West of Montgomery. The Long Wharf was built in 1848 from the bank in the middle of the block between Sacramento and Clay Streets, where Leidesdorff Street now is, 800 feet into the bay. After 1850 the Wharf was extended 2,000 feet and the Pacific Mail steamers and other large vessels anchored there. Long Wharf is now Commercial Street.

SITE OF FIRST U.S. BRANCH MINT IN CALIFORNIA. Commercial between Montgomery and Kearny. The first United States branch mint in San Francisco was authorized by Congress July 3, 1852, and opened for operation April 3, 1854. Although altered, the building still stands today.

SITE OF FORT GUNNYBAGS. Sacramento between Davis and Front. Site of the headquarters of the Vigilance Committee of 1856, Fort Gunnybags was so named when Judge David S. Terry was arrested and confined to a cell here. The Committee, fearing that the Judge's friends might attempt a jail break, decided to fortify their building. Their method—gunnysacks filled with sand.

SHORE LINE MARKER. Battery, Bush, and Market. This site marks the shore line of San Francisco Bay at the time of the gold discovery in California in 1848.

SITE OF CALIFORNIA THEATER. 444 Bush. A plaque marks the site of the California Theater which raised its first curtain January 18, 1869. Built by banker William C. Ralston, the theater was a brilliant center of drama, headlining such famous artists as John Broughan, Edwin Booth, Adelaide Neilson, and Lotta Crabtree.

of the Bay Area

RINCON HILL. First Street between Harrison and Bryant. Lowest of San Francisco's hills, Rincon Hill first served as a government reserve (protected by a battery of cannons), and secondly as a marine hospital, and was once a most fashionable residential district.

SITE OF WOODWARD'S GARDENS. Mission and Duboce. San Francisco's most popular resort during 1866–1892, Woodward's Gardens was an amusement park catering to all tastes. The Gardens occupied the block bounded by Mission, Duboce, Valencia, and 14th Streets.

MISSION SAN FRANCISCO DE ASIS (MISSION DOLORES). 16th and Dolores. San Francisco de Asis, founded in 1776 by Father Junipero Serra, was sixth in the chain of missions. Although Mission Dolores, which took its name from the nearby stream Arroyo de los Dolores, lacks the customary arches, arcades, and towers, its charm lies in its massive simplicity.

ORIGINAL SITE OF THE BANCROFT LIBRARY. 1538 Valencia Street, San Francisco. On this site, from 1881 to 1906, stood the library of Hubert Howe Bancroft, who in 1860 began collecting the wealth of material which was to subsequently result in the writing of his monumental history of western North America. In 1905 the library was purchased by the University of California and a year later was moved to the Berkeley campus.

SAN MATEO COUNTY

BRODERICK-TERRY DUELING PLACE. South end of Lake Merced. It was on this ground in the early morning of Tuesday, September 13, 1859, that U.S. Senator David C. Broderick was fatally wounded by Judge David S. Terry in a duel.

PORTOLA EXPEDITION CAMP. Pacifica, San Pedro Valley. Gaspar de Portola's 1769 expedition camped near San Pedro Creek from October 31 to November 3. Scouting parties brought news to the camp of a large body of water (San Francisco Bay) to the east.

SANCHEZ ADOBE. Off Linda Mar Boulevard, Pacifica. Francisco Sanchez (1805–1862), grantee of the 8,926 acre Rancho San Pedro, and alcalde of San Francisco and Commandante of Militia under the Mexican Republic, built this fine adobe in 1842–46. After Sanchez's death, his home was purchased and remodeled by General Edward Kirkpatrick. In 1947 the County of San Mateo bought and restored the house, which now serves as a public museum.

SITE OF DISCOVERY OF SAN FRANCISCO BAY. Sweeney Ridge, above San Andreas Lake. On November 4, 1769, Captain Gaspar de Portola—having received news from his scouts of a body of water to the east—climbed to the summit of Sweeney Ridge and beheld San Francisco Bay for the first time.

ANZA EXPEDITION CAMP. El Camino Real at Howard, Burlingame. The Juan Bautista de Anza Expedition of 1776, on their way up the Peninsula to select sites for the mission and presidio of San Francisco, camped here on March 26 at a dry watercourse just beyond Arroyo de San Mateo.

"THE HOSPICE" (OUTPOST OF MISSION DOLORES). Southwest corner of Baywood and El Camino Real, San Mateo. The Mission Hospice, built by the Spanish padres around 1800, served as an overnight stopping place for travelers, and as a center for the mission's farming operation.

PORTOLA EXPEDITION CAMP. 3.8 miles south of Half Moon Bay on Ocean Shore Road. The Portola Expedition of 1769 camped on the south bank of Purisima Creek October 27. An army engineer with the Portola party labeled the Indian village on the north bank of the creek "Las Pulgas," because the soldiers who occupied some abandoned Indian huts were literally covered with fleas.

WOODSIDE STORE. Tripp Road and Kings Mountain Road, 1.5 miles northwest of Woodside. Built in 1854 among sawmills and redwood groves by Dr. R. O. Tripp and M. A. Parkhurst, the general store was operated by Dr. Tripp himself until his death in 1909. The County of San Mateo purchased the store in 1940 and operates it as a public museum.

SITE OF THE FORMER VILLAGE OF SEARSVILLE. Sand Hill Road and Portola Road, Woodside. Here was the lumberman's village of Searsville, named after its first settler, John L. Sears, who arrived in 1854. Across the road westerly from the present site marker was a hotel; to the southeast were a school, a blacksmith shop, and dwellings. In 1891 the buildings were removed as water rose behind a new dam.

SITE OF SAN MATEO COUNTY'S FIRST SAW MILL. Portola Road near La Honda Road, .3 mile south of Woodside. About 300 feet south of the present site marker, on the banks of Alambique Creek, stood San Mateo County's first saw mill, built by Charles Brown in 1847. The mill was run by water power and was similar in structure to Sutter's Mill at Coloma.

OLD STORE AT LA HONDA. Highway 84, La Honda. In the winter of 1861–62, John L. Sears settled in the mountains 17 miles from Redwood City—and called the place La Honda. Here he constructed a store which was often referred to as "Bandit Built Store." The story goes that Sears employed two newcomers—Jim and Bob Younger—who afterwards were proven members of the James Boys' gang. Although not the original building, the store is still in use today on the old site.

SANTA CLARA COUNTY

OLD ADOBE. 3260 The Alameda, Santa Clara. This adobe, among the oldest in Santa Clara Valley, was one of several continuous rows of homes built from 1782 to 1800 as dwellings for Mission Santa Clara's Indians. Today this historical landmark is used by the Santa Clara Women's Club for its clubhouse.

SITE OF SANTA CLARA MISSION. Santa Clara University, The Alameda, Santa Clara. Third and last site of the Santa Clara Mission, it was dedicated in 1822 in the "Valley of the Oaks." The mission functioned as such until 1851 when it became Santa Clara College.

MORELAND SCHOOL. Payne and Saratoga, Campbell. Established in 1851, this is the oldest known rural school district in California. In 1852 the home of Zachariah Moreland was used for the school house, and it is in his honor that the district was so named.

PAUL MASSON MOUNTAIN WINERY. Pierce Road, Saratoga. On this site the Frenchman Paul Masson established his vineyards in the 1880's. The original sandstone walls and a 12th-century Spanish Romanesque portal, transferred here from St. Joseph's Church in San Jose after the 1906 earthquake, still stand.

TOWN OF SARATOGA. Saratoga. Anza's exploring party passed through this area in 1776, but it was lumbering which brought the settlers to Saratoga in the 1850's. Other industries established here were: a lime quarry, a grist mill, a tannery, a paper mill, and a pasteboard mill.

FORBES FLOUR MILL. Between Old Town Pedestrian Bridge and Church Street, Los Gatos. Here are the remains of the four-story stone flour mill built in 1854 by James Alexander Forbes. The town which grew around this building was first called Forbes Mill, then Forbestown, and finally Los Gatos.

VASQUEZ TREE AND SITE OF 21-MILE HOUSE. 1.25 miles south of Morgan Hill on U.S. 101. Passengers on the Monterey-San Jose stagecoach run revived themselves at the famous stage station, "21-Mile House," which stood under a lone oak. The tree reportedly got its name from the bandit Vasquez, who tied his horse to the tree while he spent his loot in the station.

FIRST SITE OF EL PUEBLO DE SAN JOSE DE GUADALUPE. Jefferson School grounds, San Jose. Lieutenant Jose Moraga

...Historical Landmarks of the Bay Area

and fourteen families founded El Pueblo de San Jose de Guadalupe (or San Jose) on or near this spot in 1777.

SITE OF CALIFORNIA'S FIRST STATE CAPITAL. 100 block South Market, San Jose. Directly opposite the present marker was the first State Capitol Building in which California's first legislature assembled in December, 1849. San Jose was the seat of state government from 1849 until 1851, when the capital was moved to Vallejo.

NEW ALMADEN MINE. 11 miles south of San Jose off Almaden Expressway between U.S. 101 and State 82. This cinnabar hill was most productive—first the Indians used its pigment for paint, and then miners mined for mercury. When gold was discovered and mercury became indispensable for extracting the yellow metal, the mine became world famous. In 1864 it was sold for $1,700,000.

ALMADEN VINEYARDS. Kooser Road, south of San Jose. On this site in 1852 Charles Le-Franc made the first commercial plantings of fine European wine grapes (which he imported from France around Cape Horn) in Santa Clara County and founded Almaden Vineyards.

ALAMEDA COUNTY

MISSION SAN JOSE. State Highway 21, Fremont. Founded in 1797 by Father Fermin Lasuen and Sergeant Pedro Amador, Mission San Jose was the fourteenth mission and one of the most prosperous. Except for part of the padres' quarters, the mission was completely destroyed in the earthquake of 1868.

LELAND STANFORD WINERY. Holy Name Road, Mission San Jose. Founded by Leland Stanford in 1869, the restored buildings and winery are now occupied by Weibel Champagne Vineyards.

VALLEJO FLOUR MILL. North of Niles Canyon Road, Niles. The town of Niles grew up around the flour mill built in 1853 by Jose de Jesus Vallejo, brother of General Vallejo. Now part of the Fremont communities, Niles was once known as "Vallejo Mills."

SITE OF FIRST COUNTY COURT HOUSE. Union City (Alvarado). Alameda's first county government met on this site in 1853 in a two-story wooden building originally constructed for a merchandise store. Three years later, following a vote of the people, the county seat was moved to San Leandro.

ESTUDILLO HOME. 550 Estudillo, San Leandro. Jose Joaquin Estudillo's home, built in 1850, was only one of three buildings standing in San Leandro in 1866. The Estudillo family founded San Leandro and donated several lots to the city.

ALAMEDA TERMINAL OF THE FIRST TRANSCONTINENTAL RAILROAD. Foot of Pacific, Alameda. Railroad work was begun at Niles in 1869 so the Eastern railroads could reach the Bay Area. That same year the first Central Pacific train reached San Francisco Bay at Alameda.

JOAQUIN MILLER HOME. Joaquin Miller Road and Sanborn Drive, Oakland. The eccentric Miller, a poet of the West, resided on his estate "The Hights" from 1886 to 1913. His studio home "The Abby," in which he wrote perhaps his most famous verse, "Columbus," is still standing. Miller personally built a platform for his funeral pyre, and monuments to General John C. Fremont, Robert Browning, and Moses, all of which are still intact. In 1919 the city of Oakland purchased the estate; it is now Joaquin Miller Park.

CHURCH OF ST. JAMES THE APOSTLE. 1540 12th, Oakland. This church, founded under the authority of Bishop Kip, first Episcopal Bishop for California, has given uninterrupted service to Oakland since June 27, 1858.

CRESTA BLANCA WINERY. Livermore Valley. In 1882 Charles A. Wetmore planted his vineyard in the Livermore Valley, and in 1889 he won for California, with his Cresta Blanca wine, the highest honor at the Paris Exposition. This award brought assurance to California wine growers that their wines could compare with the finest in the world.

CONCANNON VINEYARD. 2 miles southeast of Livermore. Concannon Vineyard, still in operation today, was founded by James Concannon in 1883. The quality the winery achieved in sacramental and commercial wines helped establish Livermore Valley as a select wine growing district.

CONTRA COSTA COUNTY

JOAQUIN MORAGA ADOBE. 3.9 miles from Orinda, Moraga Valley. Grandson of Jose Joaquin Moraga, founder and first commandant of San Francisco's Presidio, Don Joaquin Moraga, for whom Moraga Valley was named, was granted Rancho de los Palos Colorados in 1835. The adobe was built in 1841 and still stands today.

DON SALVIO PACHECO ADOBE. Center Plaza, Concord. In 1834 Don Salvio Pacheco was granted Monte del Diablo and a year later constructed his adobe there. The building, which has been altered, is used today as a restaurant.

DON FERNANDO PACHECO ADOBE. Grant and Solano, Concord. One quarter mile north of this intersection is the adobe house constructed by Don Fernando Pacheco in 1843. The home, completely reconstructed in 1941, is used by the Contra Costa Horseman's Association as headquarters.

VICENTE MARTINEZ ADOBE. Franklin Avenue, Martinez. In 1849 Vicente Martinez built his adobe on Rancho Pinole, land which was granted to his father, a commandant of San Francisco's Presidio in the 1840's. The Martinez house is 200 yards northwest of the John Muir house.

JOHN MUIR HOME. 4440 Alhambra Avenue, Martinez. This was the home of John Muir, noted naturalist, explorer, conservationist, and extoller of the beauties of the Sierra Nevada. Muir lived here from 1890 to 1914.

SOLANO COUNTY

BENICIA CAPITOL. First and G, Benicia. On this site is the Old State Capitol Building, built of salmon brick in 1852. Many original relics are preserved including the Doric portico pillars and the interior columns which were made from masts of discarded sailing ships. The chief founder, Robert Semple, named the town after General Vallejo's wife, Francisca Benicia.

BENICIA ARSENAL. East end, M Street, Benicia. Founded in 1851, the Benicia Arsenal was used by the U.S. Army as an ordnance depot until 1964 when the city of Benicia purchased the property for use as an industrial park. Many of the historic features, including a building dating back to 1869, have been preserved.

BENICIA SEMINARY. Benicia. Here was the site of the birthplace of Mills College, founded in 1852 as the Young Ladies Seminary of Benicia. Acquired in 1865 by Susan and Cyrus Mills, the school was moved to its present Oakland site in 1871 and was chartered as a college by the State of California in 1885.

SITE OF STATE CAPITOL AT VALLEJO. 219 York, Vallejo. Vallejo was the second seat of state government, from 1852 to 1853, before moving to Benicia. Close to this site stood the capitol building which served the 1852, 1853 State Legislatures.

FIRST NAVAL STATION IN THE PACIFIC. Mare Island Naval Shipyard, Vallejo. Established in 1854, Mare Island Naval Yard was the Navy's first shipyard, ammunition depot, hospital, Marine barracks, cemetery, chapel, and radio station in the Pacific area.

NAPA COUNTY

GRAVE OF GEORGE C. YOUNT. Yountville. George Calvert Yount (1794–1865) was the first United States citizen to be ceded a Spanish land grant in the Napa Valley (1836). A native of North Carolina, Yount was a trapper, rancher, and miller.

GEORGE YOUNT BLOCKHOUSE. 1 mile north of Yountville on State 29. In this area George Yount constructed a log blockhouse in 1836. Close to the blockhouse, which was the first non-Indian dwelling in Napa County, were Yount's adobe, grist, and saw mills.

OLD BALE MILL. 3 miles northwest of St. Helena. Built in 1846 by Dr. E. T. Bale, this grist mill was at the convenience of all nearby residents who needed grain ground into meal. The inside of the mill is not open at present, but a small area alongside the wheel is a county park and makes a delightful spot for picnicking.

CHARLES KRUG WINERY. Krug Ranch, St. Helena. Founded in 1861 by Charles Krug, this is the oldest operating winery in the Napa Valley. The chateau type estate is open for touring and one of the original relics on display is the small cider press Krug used for making his first wine.

BERINGER BROTHERS WINERY. St. Helena. Beringer Brothers Winery has been in continuous operation since its construction in 1876 by Frederick and Jacob Beringer. Chinese laborers built the winery and dug through limestone hills to make wine-aging tunnels. The temperature within the tunnels averages 58 degrees, and never varies more than 2 degrees summer or winter.

SAM BRANNAN STORE. Calistoga. Sam Brannan moved from San Francisco to the Napa Valley in 1859 and at the foot of Mount St. Helena opened a store which in one year reportedly made a total of $50,000.

SAM BRANNAN COTTAGE. Calistoga. Sam Brannan had plans to develop this area into a hotsprings resort similar to Saratoga in the East. (Calistoga is a combination of the words California and Saratoga.) In 1866, for the grand opening of the resort, Brannan had many cottages built and palm trees planted. This is the sole survivor of the cottages.

SCHRAMSBERG. 3.8 miles south of Calistoga. Founded in 1862 by Jacob Schram, a barber from Johannisberg, Germany, Schramsberg was the first hillside winery in the Napa Valley. The original house and winery, which Robert Louis Stevenson devoted a chapter to in his *Silverado Squatters*, are excellently preserved.

ROBERT LOUIS STEVENSON MEMORIAL STATE PARK. Highway 53, 3 miles northeast of Calistoga. Robert Louis Stevenson and his bride came to Silverado in 1880 and lived here for several months while he gathered notes for *Silverado Squatters*. The Napa County Women's Club erected a monument on the site of the cabin —"an open book carved in red Scotch granite, resting on a rock pedestal, with an inscription from the writer's work."

SONOMA COUNTY

BEAR FLAG MONUMENT. Northeast corner of Sonoma Plaza, Sonoma. The bronze monument of a bear waving the Bear Flag was erected to commemorate the raising of the Bear Flag by the Bear Flag Party on June 14, 1846, to declare California free from Mexican rule. The Bear Flag flew only about a month, and in July it was replaced with the American Flag.

GENERAL M.G. VALLEJO HOME. West Spain and Third Street West, Sonoma. Constructed of adobe brick covered with wood, this house was named Lachryma Montis (tear of the mountain) after a natural spring in the area. General M. G. Vallejo, commander of the northern Mexican frontier, founder of the Pueblo of Sonoma, and a member of the first Constitutional Convention of California, occupied the home from 1850 to 1890.

NASH ADOBE. 579 First Street East, Sonoma. Built in 1847, this house was where John H. Nash was taken prisoner by Lieutenant William T. Sherman in July, 1847, when he refused to relinquish his post as alcalde. The house has been completely restored.

SAMUELE SEBASTIANI VINEYARD AND WINERY. Spain Street, Sonoma. In 1825 the Franciscan Fathers from the Sonoma Mission used this land to plant the first vineyards in the Sonoma Valley. First the grapes were used for making sacramental wine, and later, under General Vallejo, for producing prize-winning wines. In the early 1900's Samuele Sebastiani, a young Italian immigrant, purchased the winery which his family still operates.

TEMELEC HALL. 3 miles southeast of Sonoma. This hall was erected in 1858 by Captain Granville P. Swift, a member of the Bear Flag Party. The building is constructed of stone quarried by native Indian labor.

BUENA VISTA VINICULTURAL WINERY. 2 miles northeast of Sonoma. Agoston Haraszthy, a Hungarian nobleman, in 1857 established his Buena Vista Vineyards. Visitors to the winery today can see the tunnels dug by Chinese laborers, part of the old stone winery, and original equipment.

MISSION SAN FRANCISCO SOLANO. 114 East Spain, Sonoma. Last and northernmost of the missions, Mission San Francisco Solano was founded in 1823 by Padre Jose Altmire. The present church, constructed in 1840 to replace an earlier wooden structure, is a complete restoration.

BLUE WING INN. 133 East Spain, Sonoma. Constructed by General Mariano Guadalupe Vallejo about 1840 to accommodate emigrants and travelers, the Inn was purchased during Gold Rush days by two retired seafaring men and run as a hotel and store. The Inn boasts such notable guests as Kit Carson, John C. Fremont, U.S. Grant, Governor Pio Pico, and William T. Sherman.

PRESIDIO OF SONOMA (SONOMA BARRACKS). Spain at First, Sonoma. The Sonoma Barracks, erected in 1836 by General Vallejo, were headquarters first for the Mexican Army, then for the Bear Flag Party, and lastly for American troops.

JACK LONDON STATE HISTORIC PARK. Glen Ellen. The "House of Happy Walls," built in 1919 by Charmain K. London in memory of her husband, Jack London, contains a recreation of his study, a large collection of his books, and artifacts gathered by the Londons on their travels. Also in the park are the ruins of "Wolf House" and London's grave.

LUTHER BURBANK HOME AND GARDEN. 200 block on Santa Rosa Avenue, Santa Rosa. A native of Massachusetts, Luther Burbank had discovered the "Burbank potato" by the time he reached Santa Rosa in 1875. Three years later he acquired his Santa Rosa gardens where great varieties of fruits, vegetables, flowers, and shrubs were produced and shipped all over the world. Recently the gardens were redesigned to show the plants Burbank developed.

ITALIAN SWISS COLONY WINERY. Asti. Here in 1881 Italian Swiss immigrants from San Francisco established an agricultural colony. The communal idea did not work, but the colony was organized into a company which took old world grape plantings and began producing choice wines.

FORT ROSS. State Highway 1, 13 miles north of Jenner. Lured to Fort Ross because of the good sea otter and fur seal hunting, the Russians founded this town in 1812. Among the historical buildings restored are the chapel (built in 1828), the commandant's quarters, and the stockade.

PETALUMA ADOBE. 4 miles east of Petaluma. This adobe, built by General Vallejo in 1834, served as headquarters for his 66,000 acre Rancho Petaluma.

LIME KILNS. 4.2 miles south of Olema. When the Russians occupied the Sonoma area (around 1812) it is reported that their stone masons built lime kilns which were worked by the Indians.

PIONEER PAPER MILL. Samuel P. Taylor State Park, ten miles west of San Anselmo. This is the site of the first paper mill on the Pacific Coast. Built in 1856 by Samuel Taylor, the mill was operated by water and then by steam power until it closed in 1884.

MISSION SAN RAFAEL ARCANGEL. Fifth and Court, San Rafael. Established in 1817 by the Franciscan Order, Mission San Rafael Arcangel was twentieth in the chain of 21 missions. The mission has been completely reconstructed on its original site.

FIRST SAWMILL IN MARIN COUNTY. Cascade Drive, Mill Valley. John Reed, who built the first house in Sausalito, and the first ferry boat that plied San Francisco Bay, also built the first sawmill in Marin on this site in 1833-34.

SITE OF THE LIGHTER WHARF AT BOLINAS. 2 miles north of Bolinas. Constructed in the 1850's, this wharf was the loading dock for lumber which was placed on lighters, which in turn were floated out to deeper water where the timber was transferred to sea-going vessels.

HOSPITAL COVE, ANGEL ISLAND. San Francisco Bay. This was the spot at which Lieutenant Juan Manuel de Ayala, commander of the first Spanish ship to enter the Golden Gate, later anchored the *San Carlos*. During his 44-day stay, in 1775, Ayala named the island La Isla de Nuestra Senora de los Angeles. The island is now a state park.

The lack of any standard bibliography of San Franciscana must puzzle literate newcomers to the Pacific Coast. Doubtless they ascribe the absence of such a reading list to the sheer impossibility of compiling an eclectic bibliography from such a volume of titles, from such literary largesse. The quantity *is* awesome. But, more likely, the lack is symptomatic of the unevenness and mediocrity of much of the writing about San Francisco, rather than its volume.

The city seems unique in being able to charm no-nonsense writers as completely as open-mouthed romantics. It is not merely the usual matter of poets sacrificing truth for a good stanza, a weakness which Plato long ago decried. Writers are enchanted, bewitched by the city of the myth-makers. It is as if the moon never sets in San Francisco.

Luckily, some writers are either immune to the witchery of San Francisco or have sufficiently de-witched themselves to be able to write objectively of a city of great color and interest, a city which needs no gilding and no bunking. They write about San Francisco as they would about London, Cape Cod, or the Great Smokies. Even when they work in the most popular field of what might be called "histalgia," a cross between history and nostalgia, they employ the necessary skills of research and interpretation as well as narration. They write about a real city. About real men, not myths. The results are apparent to critical readers of Californiana. Casual readers, too, can learn the difference between Samuel Dickson and Oscar Lewis, Stephen Longstreet and William Bronson. To help them, I have annotated the entries in the bibliography which follows. You do not have to be an expert to learn to appreciate the difference between those writers who merely resuscitate or borrow old stories and those who dig up new material in an attempt to make a genuine contribution to the chronicle of San Francisco.

Among the authors omitted you may find some old favorites whose works have simply become too dated to list. An example would be Basil Woon, whose *San Francisco and the Golden Empire* was largely a guidebook to another world—the Bay Area in 1935.

I have deliberately left out many good books which are either rare or so uncommon that they would be hard to find even in the city's antiquarian bookshops. I had hoped to list few out-of-print books, too, but because books are treated as commodities in the United States this was impossible. A given title has as short a life as a particular year's model of automobile, the paperback revolution notwithstanding. Thus, the designation o.p. signifies out-of-print and the title must be sought at antiquarian bookshops.

The following list is, of course, a personal selection. But it will be of value if it does no more than to cause San Franciscans, real and vicarious, to discipline their reading and to re-examine the mythology of the town.

Richard Dillon

GENERAL

Bancroft, Hubert H. *History of California*. San Francisco, Bancroft, 1884–90. 7 vols. o.p. *The* history of California, shot through with references to San Francisco, of course, but the seven volumes can be heavy going.

Carlisle, Henry C. *San Francisco Street Names*. San Francisco, American Trust Co., 1954. o.p. A little give-away pamphlet with much information on the naming of the city's streets. Illustrations by Mallette Dean.

Dobie, Charles C. *San Francisco: a Pageant*. New York, Appleton-Century, 1933. o.p. A romantic study of San Francisco. Graceful writing enhanced by superb drawings of E. H. Suydam, one of the artists (with Pennell and Peixotto) most successful in capturing the city's charm.

———. *San Francisco Chinatown*. New York, Appleton-Century, 1936. o.p. A companion volume to the above, again illustrated by Suydam.

Hogan, William, and William German, Eds. *The San Francisco Chronicle Reader*. New York, McGraw-Hill, 1962. o.p. An interesting sampler of the better journalism of the Monarch of the Dailies, including the bylines of Brier, Kentfield, Delaplane, Beebe, O'Flaherty, and Hoppe.

Jackson, Joseph Henry, Ed. *San Francisco Murders*. New York, Duell, Sloan & Pearce, 1947. o.p. A collection of true homicides selected and recounted by Jackson, Oscar Lewis, Lenore G. Offord, Anthony Boucher, and others.

———, Ed. *Western Gate*. New York, Farrar, Straus & Young, 1952. Subtitled "A San Francisco Reader," this is a collection of choice excerpts from everyone from Richard Henry Dana to Ernest Gann. Jackson was attempting to pin down the city's special quality in these viewpoints.

Kinnaird, Lawrence. *History of the Greater San Francisco Bay Region*.

New York, Lewis, 1966. 3 vols. $75. Volumes I and II contain the ex-University of California professor's sweeping history; volume III is a genealogical mugbook. A successor to similar huge sets of history and collective-biography by John P. Young (1912), Millard Bailey (1924), and Oscar Lewis and L. Byington (1931).

Lewis, Oscar. *San Francisco: Mission to Metropolis*. Berkeley, Howell-North, 1966. $6.95. The best history of the city available. Succinct and well illustrated.

EARLIEST DAYS (1542-1848)

Bolton, Herbert E. *Outpost of Empire*. New York, Knopf, 1939. o.p. The famous Berkeley professor's definitive book on the founding of San Francisco by the Anza expeditions, 1774–76. Scholarly but readable.

Englehardt, Zephyrn. *San Francisco, or Mission Dolores*. Chicago, Franciscan Herald Press, 1924. Out of date, hard to find; we need a good book on Mission San Francisco de Asis.

Treutlein, Theodore. *Discovery and Colonization of San Francisco Bay*. San Francisco, Calif. Historical Soc., 1969. $10. A fine new addition to the pioneering work of men like George Davidson and Henry Wagner. Much on the expeditions of Fages, Crespi, Anza, Rivera. and Palou.

GOLDEN ERA (1848-1906)

Altrocchi, Julia Cooley. *The Spectacular San Franciscans*. New York, Dutton, 1949. o.p. A volume in the Society in America Series by the author of *Snow Covered Wagons*. Much on what librarians would call the city's "social life and customs."

Asbury, Herbert. *The Barbary Coast*. New York, Putnams, 1969. $7.50. Just now back in print, this is the grand-daddy of all the underworld-San Francisco exposés—and still the best.

Atherton, Gertrude. *My San Francisco*. Indianapolis, Bobbs, Merrill, 1946. o.p. Subtitled "A Wayward Biography," it is part history of San Francisco and part autobiography of the California authoress. (Unkind reviewers called it "polished prattle" when it appeared.)

Bancroft, Hubert H. *Popular Tribunals*. San Francisco, Bancroft, 1890. 2 vols. o.p. Absolutely fascinating criminal annals of San Francisco and thereabouts, jammed with details and anecdotes.

Barth, Gunther. *Bitter Strength*. Cambridge, Harvard, 1964. $5.95. The most scholarly treatment of San Francisco's Chinese, by a UC-Berkeley history professor. For additional reading, see library card-catalog entries for Rose Hum Lee, S. W. Kung, Alexander McLeod, Betty Lee Sung.

Bean, Walton. *Boss Ruef's San Francisco*. Berkeley, University of California, 1952. $7.50. Scholarly but readable account of the Union Labor Party and Abe Ruef's empire of graft, which was interrupted by the 1906 quake and fire. See also Lately Thomas' book in this bibliography.

Beebe, Lucius, and Charles Clegg. *San Francisco's Golden Era*. Berkeley, Howell-North, 1960. $5.95. Completely fascinating antique pictures and sparkling text, put together by the inimitable Beebe.

———. *Cable Car Carnival*. Oakland, Grahame Hardy, 1951. o.p. An extra-illustrated, amusing account of the city of "the cables"; a companion volume to Edgar Kahn's less flamboyant account.

Bruce, John R. *Gaudy Century*. New York, Random House, 1948. o.p. A century of robust San Francisco journalism amusingly surveyed by the (then) City Editor of the *Chronicle*. Stewart Holbrook and Joseph Henry Jackson found it fascinating.

Bryant, Edwin. *What I Saw in California*. Palo Alto, Lewis Osborne, 1968. o.p. One of the true classics of Californiana, happily brought back in a new edition—only to go out of print almost immediately. Bryant covered all of California, including San Francisco, in 1846. Excellent on-the-spot description.

Camp, William M. *San Francisco, Port of Gold*. Garden City, New York, Doubleday, 1947. o.p. A lively, salty history of the city in windjammer days, the equal of Felix Riesenberg's volume—which is high praise. The best thing to come out of the long-forgotten Seaport Series by Doubleday.

Clarke, Dwight L. *William Tecumseh Sherman: Gold Rush Banker*. San Francisco, Calif. Historical Soc., 1969. A chronicle of the famous Union general's banking days in San Francisco before the Civil War.

Coblentz, Stanton A. *Villians and Vigilantes*. New York, Thomas Yoseloff, 1957. $5.00. Mill Valley's poet laureate attempts to explain the Vigilante movement, with some success. From James King of William's point of view, inevitably.

on San Francisco

Cowan, Robert E. *The Forgotten Characters of Old San Francisco*. Los Angeles, Ward Ritchie, 1964. o.p. A handsome book by the son of a great San Francisco bookman, largely on Emperor Norton. The only other major source, Allen Lane's *Emperor Norton, the Mad Monarch*, is also o.p. Hostile critics called Cowan's book "San Franciscolatry."

Davis, William Heath. *Seventy-Five Years in California*. San Francisco, Howell, 1967. $27.50. A wonderful picture of pioneer California, including San Francisco, by an active participant in its early history.

DeFord, Miriam A. *They Were San Franciscans*. Caldwell, Idaho, Caxton, 1941. o.p. Like the works of Cora Older, Gertrude Atherton, and others, this is gossipy local history in the form of biographical sketching, usually. Included are such folk as the eccentric millionaire James Lick, author Henry George *(Progress and Poverty)*, and the illiterate impresario, Tom Maguire.

Dillon, Richard. *Embarcadero*. New York, Coward McCann, 1960. o.p. Non-fiction yarn spinning; a collection of true tales of the San Francisco waterfront and of the men and ships calling there in the days of sail.

————. *The Hatchet Men*. New York, Coward McCann, 1962. $5.95. The only full book about the deadly tong wars of Chinatown's alleys in the late 19th century, of the reign of terror of the highbinders, and of the integration of the community after the application of socio-political reforms.

————. *Shanghaiing Days*. New York, Coward McCann, 1961. o.p. The only book on shanghaiing (kidnapping merchant seamen), which began in San Francisco and was only stamped out with the rise of Andrew Furuseth and the sailors' unions.

Duke, Thomas S. *Celebrated Criminal Cases*. San Francisco, Barry, 1910. A wonderful casebook but elusive, almost impossible to find except in the best antiquarian bookshops. To be read with Fanning and with Bancroft's *Popular Tribunals*.

Fanning, Pete. *Great Crimes of the West*, 1929. o.p. Almost as good—and almost as hard to find—as Duke (above).

Genthe, Arnold, and William Irwin. *Old Chinatown*. New York, Mitchell Kennerly, 1913. A classic photo-essay of Chinatown before the Fire by San Francisco's greatest early camera artist.

Gentry, Curt. *The Madams of San Francisco*. Garden City, New York, Doubleday, 1964. o.p. A century of naughty San Francisco, viewed from a parlor house window. Asbury-like history marred by somewhat too many minor errors of fact.

Harlan, George H. *San Francisco Ferryboats*. Berkeley, Howell-North, 1967. $7.50. The definitive book on the ferries, with lots of historical pictures. Maritime history collectors will also want his earlier (1951) *Of Walking Beams and Paddle Wheels* (o.p.).

Harpending, Asbury. *The Great Diamond Hoax*. Norman, University of Oklahoma, 1958. $2.95. Adventures and apologia by a colorful San Francisco adventurer, including the story of his outfitting a Confederate raider on the Embarcadero during the Civil War.

Holdredge, Helen. *Firebelle Lillie*. New York, Meredith, 1967. $6.95. The best book on the colorful lady fire buff, memorialized by Coit Tower, Lillie Hitchcock Coit.

————. *Mammy Pleasant*. San Carlos, Nourse, 1961. $5.00. Probably the author's best book, an interesting account of a *femme fatale* of old San Francisco accused of everything up to and including voodoo. A contribution to San Francisco Negro history.

Jacobson, Pauline. *City of the Golden Fifties*. Berkeley, University of California, 1941. o.p. "Histalgia" again, evolved from the journalist-author's contributions to the San Francisco *Bulletin* around World War I.

Johnson, Kenneth, Ed. *San Francisco As It Is*. Georgetown, California, Talisman Press, 1964. A collection of human interest columns from the *enfant terrible* of 1850–52 San Francisco journalism, the *Picayune*. Fine local color; a very handsome book from a fine press.

Jones, Idwal. *Ark of Empire*. Garden City, New York, Doubleday, 1951. o.p. A born story-teller, Jones uses the old Montgomery Block, home of artists, Sutro Library, and Duncan Nicol's bar as a focus for stories of men of the good old days.

Kahn, Edgar M. *Cable Car Days*. Stanford, Stanford University Press, 1944. $4.50. The standard book on Andrew Hallidie's cable cars.

Kemble, John Haskell. *San Francisco Bay: A Pictorial Maritime History*. Cambridge, Md., Cornell Maritime Press, 1957. o.p. Technically out of print, this turns up in "remainder" book stores as the best bargain of the year, from time to time. Kemble is perhaps the best maritime historian on the Coast; the illustrations are first-rate.

Kroninger, Robert H. *Sarah and the Senator*. Berkeley, Howell-North, 1964. $5.95. A judge attempts to unravel the knotty history of nabob William Sharon, Sarah Hill, and firebrand Judge David Terry. A *cause celebre* of old San Francisco.

Levy, Harriet L. *920 O'Farrell Street*. Garden City, New York, Doubleday, 1947. o.p. An affectionate, charming autobiographical reminiscence of comfortable Jewish society in San Francisco before the Fire, illustrated by Mallette Dean.

Lewis, Oscar. *Big Four*. New York, Knopf, 1938. $6.50. The fascinating story of Central Pacific Railroad nabobs Charles Crocker, Leland Stanford, C. P. Huntington, and Mark Hopkins. Probably the best of Lewis' many fine books.

————. *Silver Kings*. New York, Knopf, 1947. A sort of sequel to *Big Four*, this is an account of the silver barons who brought a transfusion of new wealth to San Francisco from the Comstock Lode—John Mackay, James G. Fair, James Flood, and William S. O'Brien.

————. *This Was San Francisco*. New York, David McKay, 1962. o.p. Lewis ties together with a narrative thread old accounts of San Francisco by Bierce, Kipling, Jessie Fremont, and folk of that ilk.

————, and Carroll D. Hall. *Bonanza Inn*. New York, Knopf, 1939. $5.95. The entertaining and informative biography of the West's great hostelry, the Palace Hotel.

Megquier, Mary Jane. *Apron Full of Gold*. San Marino, Huntington Library, 1949. $3.50. A collection of letters from San Francisco, 1849–56, giving the flavor of the place.

Myers, John Myers. *San Francisco's Reign of Terror*. Garden City, New York, Doubleday, 1968. o.p. Slangy, flippant, but a book which rescues the story of Judge Ned McGowan, the Vigilance Committee's Number One Target and, therefore, is worth having.

O'Brien, Robert. *This Is San Francisco*. New York, Whittlesey House, 1948. o.p. A collection of true stories by a gifted raconteur whose column "Riptides" brightened the *Chronicle* during its Paul Smith hey-day. (Also recommended is his o.p. *California Called Them*, 1954.)

Riesenberg, Felix, Jr. *Golden Gate*. New York, Knopf, 1940. o.p. Like W. M. Camp's book, this is history flecked with salt spray, written by a man who once "covered the waterfront" for the San Francisco *News*. The story of the harbor from 1769 to 1939.

Rourke, Constance. *Troupers of the Gold Coast*. New York, Harcourt, Brace, 1928. o.p. Pioneer California theater history has been neglected by writers after an excellent beginning by this author. Not restricted to San Francisco, but the city, of course, dominated early California theater. Much of the book is on the rise of Lola Montez's discovery, Lotta Crabtree.

Soule, Frank, and others. *The Annals of San Francisco*. Palo Alto, Lewis Osborne, 1966. $26.00. A new edition of this essential book—teeming with information, well illustrated—on San Francisco to 1854. It has a useful introduction, an index, and notes on the illustrations.

Stewart, George R. *Committee of Vigilance*. Boston, Houghton Mifflin, 1964. $5.00. Not the best book, by far, of this popular California historian, yet it is probably the best thing we have on the Vigilance Committee of 1851, so controversial and difficult is the subject. Pro-Committee survey of the 100 days when citizens took the law into their own hands to clean up the Sydney Ducks and other criminals.

Taper, Bernard, Ed. *Mark Twain's San Francisco*. New York, McGraw-Hill, 1963. o.p. Very little editing or interpretation; mostly a collection of Sam Clemens' items on San Francisco, like the hard-to-find (1938) *Washoe Giant in San Francisco*.

Taylor, Bayard. *Eldorado*. Palo Alto, Lewis Osborne, 1968. 2 vols. $21.00. A classic by one of 19th-century America's best writers. The Zamorano Club bibliophiles of Los Angeles termed it "probably the outstanding book on the early gold rush in California." Not restricted to San Francisco, of course. This new edition has added material, including a biographical introduction.

Thomas, Lately. *Debonair Scoundrel*. New York, Holt, Rinehart & Winston, 1962. o.p. It is hard to choose between this book on Abe Ruef and Walton Bean's volume. The latter is a scholar; Thomas is a *nom de plume*d ex-newspaperman.

Valentine, Alan. *Vigilante Justice*. New York, Reynald and Hitchcock, 1956. o.p. A briskly told account of the two Vigilance movements, 1851 and 1856, and thus useful since George Stewart discusses only the former and John M. Myers the latter.

... Selected Readings on San Francisco

Walker, Franklin. *San Francisco's Literary Frontier*. New York, Knopf, 1939. o.p. A genuine contribution to history, this is a well-written survey of the literary scene of the city with emphasis on the 1860's and that period's stars—Twain, Harte, Mulford, Coolbrith, Stoddard, Miller, George, Bierce. Most highly recommended.

Wells, Evelyn. *Champagne Days of San Francisco*. Garden City, New York, Doubleday, 1947. o.p. A delightful, anecdotal history of the period from the Gay Nineties through the Fire. Much on the social and literary and bohemian life. The Mauve Decade with champagne and roses.

Wilson, Carol Green. *Chinatown Quest*. Stanford, Stanford University Press, 1950. o.p. The life and adventures of Lo Mo, Donaldina Cameron, the Presbyterian crusader who cleaned Chinatown of its vicious traffic in sing-song girls before the Quake.

Wilson, Neill C. *Here Is the Golden Gate*. New York, Morrow, 1962. o.p. Similar to Riesenberg, Camp, and *Embarcadero*; tales of the most colorful port in America by an old hand at writing.

Writers Project. California. (American Guide Series) *San Francisco: The Bay and Its Cities*. New York, Hastings House, 1947. $8.95. Though badly dated, even in the revised edition, this book remains essential for any student or collector of San Franciscana. The best place to start when building a San Francisco bookshelf.

PORTRAIT OF A CITY (1906-1946)

Bronson, William. *The Earth Shook, The Sky Burned*. Garden City, New York, Doubleday, 1959. $6.95. More than a picture book, this is a lavishly illustrated history of the 1906 Earthquake and Fire.

Brown, Allen. *Golden Gate, Biography of a Bridge*. Garden City, New York, Doubleday, 1965. o.p. The only real book on the stupendous Golden Gate Bridge.

Coffman, William. *American in the Rough*. New York, Simon & Shuster, 1955. o.p. An autobiography of a San Francisco businessman and Shrine leader which throws much light on the rough and tumble history of the Embarcadero during the dying days of sail.

Duffus, Robert L. *The Tower of Jewels*. New York, Norton, 1960. o.p. Not a history of the Panama Pacific Exposition, despite its title, but an autobiographical memoir of a newspaperman's seven years on Fremont Older's *Bulletin* during a period of changing times.

Gentry, Curt. *Frame Up*. New York, Norton, 1967. $7.50. The Mooney-Billings Case was the Sacco-Vanzetti affair of San Francisco. Hysteria and perjury apparently played a part, and Gentry is convinced of the two accused parade-bombers' innocence. Honestly researched and told.

Kennedy, John Castillo. *The Great Earthquake and Fire*. New York, Morrow, 1963. $5.00. Like Miss Sutherland's, below, a title to add if you already have Bronson's book on the Quake.

Lowe, Pardee. *Father and Glorious Descendant*. Boston, Little, Brown, 1951. o.p. Similar to Jade Snow Wong's book and with a strong (if smaller) following among literate San Franciscans.

Newhall, Ruth. *San Francisco's Enchanted Palace*. Berkeley, Howell-North, 1967. $7.50. A handsomely illustrated account of the Marina's Palace of Fine Arts. The author brings the story from the Panama Pacific International Exposition almost to date.

Older, Cora. *San Francisco: Magic City*. New York, David McKay, 1961. $5.95. More "histalgia," this time by Fremont Older's widow. A scrapbook of anecdotes with little of the personal touch that would have raised this above the other light, nostalgic local histories.

Sutherland, Monica. *The Damnedest Finest Ruins*. New York, Coward McCann, 1959. $3.50. A pretty good supplementary book on the Quake and Fire, by an Englishwoman.

Wilson, Carol Green. *Gump's Treasure Trade*. New York, Crowell, 1949. $8.95. The story of the Gumps and the store which made Americans jade and Orientalia-conscious, told with gusto in a new and enlarged edition.

Wong, Jade Snow. *Fifth Chinese Daughter*. New York, Harper, 1950. $4.95. A charming, autobiographical account of Chinatown from the inside written, modestly, in the third person. By one of the city's outstanding artists. In paperback, too.

CITY ON THE MOVE (1946-date)

Benet, James. *A Guide to San Francisco and the Bay Region*. New York, Random House, 1963. $6.95. A meaty and intelligent baedeker, offering much more than the usual guidebook. Of permanent interest, unlike most guides.

Caen, Herb. *Baghdad by the Bay*. Garden City, New York, Doubleday, 1951. o.p. *Don't Call It Frisco*. Garden City, New York, Doubleday, 1953. o.p. *Only in San Francisco*. Garden City, New York, Doubleday, 1960. o.p. A trilogy of impressionistic textual "snapshots" of the city, past and present, by its resident Pepys. Culled from Caen's columnar writing in the *Chronicle*.

———, and Dong Kingman. *San Francisco, City on Golden Hills*. Garden City, New York, Doubleday, 1967. $25.00. A more permanent bit of Caeniana enhanced by the artist's impressionistic illustrations—41 color plates, 29 two-tone plates, and many black and white sketches.

Chiang Yee. *The Silent Traveler in San Francisco*. New York, Norton, 1964. o.p. A fine companion-piece to Caen-Kingman, this is also an impression of San Francisco in text and art, by an Oriental visitor. The sketches are all black and white. A refreshingly detached though sympathetic view of the city.

The City. San Francisco in Pictures. San Francisco, *Chronicle*, 1961. o.p. A photo-survey of the town with an introduction by Stanton Delaplane.

Conrad, Barnaby. *San Francisco: A Profile With Pictures*. New York, Viking, 1959. A photo-essay with good text.

Doss, Margot Patterson. *San Francisco At Your Feet*. New York, Grove, 1964. $1.95. Far more than a guidebook, this paperback volume is *sui generis*. A kind of hiker's guide to scenic and historic San Francisco, it is loaded with insights.

Gentry, Curt. *The Dolphin Guide to San Francisco and the Bay Area, Present and Past*. Garden City, New York, Doubleday, 1962. $.95. A great bargain. Of permanent use since Gentry knows his history as well as geography. A *vade mecum* for all visitors.

Gilliam, Harold, and Phil Palmer. *The Face of San Francisco*. Garden City, New York, Doubleday, 1960. $6.50. Perhaps the most successful of all the text-and-photo essays on the city. Put a discerning writer and a sensitive and artistic photographer together and this is what you get.

Hills of San Francisco. San Francisco, *Chronicle*, 1959. o.p. An interesting photo-essay on the many hills of the city from the well-known to the lesser-known.

Our San Francisco. Photographs by Michael Bry and others; text by Harold Gilliam and others. San Francisco, Diablo Press, 1964. o.p. Superb photography but skimpy text. An album, not a book, but beautiful.

Palmer, Phil, and Mike Palmer. *Cable Cars of San Francisco*. Berkeley, Howell-North, 1959. $1.00. A paperback picture book on the cable cars. Quite a bargain.

Palmer, Phil, and Jim Walls. *Chinatown, San Francisco*. Berkeley, Howell-North, 1960. $1.00. The text is by Jim Walls of the *Chronicle* but the book belongs to Palmer and his camera. The best photo interpretation of Chinatown since Arnold Genthe.

Rigney, Francis, and L. Douglas Smith. *The Real Bohemians*. New York, Basic Books, 1961. o.p. Though ancient Beatnikistan with gun and camera—or, really, with psychological test and sociological fever chart. Ethnology of a vanished race, ancestral to the hippies.

Watkins, Thomas H. *San Francisco in Color*. New York, Hastings House, 1968. $4.95. A succinct and intelligent text—more than captions—accompanying fine color plates of San Francisco views. A volume in the Profiles of America Series.

———, and Roger Olmstead. *Here Today*. Chronicle Books, 1969. $14.95. The results of an amazing survey of our surviving architectural heritage, by the Junior League. The buildings are located street-by-street and many are photographed. A census and a warning. A must for anyone concerned with preserving the face of San Francisco.

NATURAL HISTORY

Gilliam, Harold. *San Francisco Bay*. Garden City, New York, Doubleday, 1957. $4.95. The book which brought Gilliam to the public's attention. The state's most informed conservationist is also one of its best writers. Highly recommended as a survey of our most priceless asset, San Francisco Bay.

———. *Weather of the San Francisco Bay Area*. Berkeley, University of California, 1962. $1.50. This small (72-page) paperback handbook is most educational. About our winds, fogs, weather, this is one of the University's California Natural History Guides.

———. *The Natural World of San Francisco*. Garden City, New York, Doubleday, 1967. $6.95. The geology, flora, and fauna of the city in Gilliam's authoritative and gifted prose, complemented by Michael Bry's splendid photographs of the environment.

Jenkins, Olaf, and others. *Geologic Guidebook of the San Francisco Bay Counties*. San Francisco, State Division of Mines, $2.50. A much too little-known volume which ranges from history to landscape to fossils. (Calif. Division of Mines Bulletin #154.)

Scott, Mellier. *San Francisco Bay Area: A Metropolis in Perspective*. Berkeley, University of California, 1959. $12.50. This labor of love, almost a decade in the writing and researching, is a kind of ecological history of the Bay Area by a gifted regional planner.

Suggs, Robert Carl. *The Archaeology of San Francisco*. New York, Crowell, 1965. $3.50. This is actually a juvenile book (grades 7–12) but it is all we have on the subject and it is not bad.

ARTS, SPORTS, CUISINE

Bloomfield, Arthur. *The San Francisco Opera*. New York, Appleton-Century-Crofts, 1962. $6.00. A history of the San Francisco Opera Association, founded (1923) by Gaetano Merola. Much detail on artists and performances.

Einstein, Charles. *A Flag For San Francisco*. New York, Simon & Shuster, 1962. $4.50. Few sports writers have either the wit or the writing skill of this author, who details the Giants' crusade for a pennant in 1961.

Kan, John J., and Charles Leong. *Eight Immortal Flavors*. Berkeley, Howell-North, 1963. $5.95. More than a cookbook, though subtitled "Secrets of Cantonese Cookery," this volume offers insights into the role of cuisine in Chinese culture.

King, Joe. *The San Francisco Giants*. Englewood Cliffs, New Jersey, Prentice Hall, 1958. o.p. A breezy view of the big leaguers by a knowledgeable sports writer.

McGuire, Dan. *San Francisco 49ers*. New York, Coward McCann, 1960. o.p. A volume in Coward McCann's Sports Library on the "always a bridesmaid" team of the NFL by a 49ers publicity director.

Mardikian, George. *Dinner at Omar Khayyam's*. New York, Viking, 1948. o.p. A book on Armenian cookery by the owner of a tourist must-see restaurant, the author of the sentimental autobiography *Song of America*.

Muscatine, Doris. *A Cook's Tour of San Francisco*. New York, Scribner, 1963. $7.50. This culinary guidebook takes you to the best San Francisco restaurants to check on their favorite recipes.

Read, R. B. *The San Francisco Underground Gourmet*. New York, Simon & Shuster, 1969. $1.95. A companion to the best selling *New York Underground Gourmet*. A guide to the city's low priced places and, incidentally, to the great variety of international cuisine in the city.

Rosenbaum, Art, and Bob Stevens. *The Giants of San Francisco*. New York, Coward McCann, 1963. o.p. Another book on the baseballers, this time by two of the city's sports writers.

Sarvis, Shirley. *Crab and Abalone*. Indianapolis, Bobbs, Merrill, 1968. $5.00. A stunning book; a collection of excellent recipes for the twin ambrosias of the West Coast—Dungeness crab and abalone—in a very handsome format designed and illustrated by Tony Calvello.

———, and Georgia Sackett. *Firehouse Favorites*. Indianapolis, Bobbs, Merrill, 1965. o.p. Hearty fare described by Misses Sarvis and Sackett and illustrated by Tony Calvello, with photos by Bruce Harlow.

FICTION

Busch, Niven. *California Street*. New York, Simon & Shuster, 1959. $4.50. The saga of a newspaper publisher, his family, and an inside power-play to grab control of the paper. Some reviewers did not think too much of it but others found it engrossing and the London *Times* compared it to the work of Dos Passos and James T. Farrell.

———. *The San Franciscans*. New York, Simon & Shuster, 1962. o.p. This novel, by the author of *Duel in the Sun*, was not as well received as *California Street*. A similar novel, about a bank in legal and financial difficulties, it won approval from San Francisco book critic William Hogan who likened Busch to John P. Marquand.

Crane, Clarkson. *The Western Shore*. New York, Harcourt, Brace, 1925. o.p. A long-forgotten book, way ahead of its day in realism, about the University of California, Berkeley, rather than San Francisco. Highly thought of by men of letters like Oscar Lewis and Lawrence Clark Powell. Perhaps worth rediscovering.

Coolbrith, Ina. *Songs From the Golden Gate*. Boston, Houghton Mifflin, 1895. o.p. A 159-page sampler of the 19th-century Poet Laureate of California. Of more historic than literary interest today.

Dobie, Charles C. *San Francisco Tales*. New York, Appleton-Century, 1935. o.p. Dobie was talented in both fiction and non-fiction. These 18 short stories cover Chinatown and the Italian quarter and show him to be a talented and polished writer, if not a deep one.

Edminston, James. *Home Again*. Garden City, New York, Doubleday, 1955. o.p. An indignant document but only a fair novel. The subject is the shocking uprooting of the Japanese-Americans during World War II and their deportation and internment.

Eyre, Katherine Wigmore. *The Chinese Box*. New York, Appleton-Century-Crofts, 1959. o.p. A story of a very social San Francisco family in the 19th century.

Forbes, Kathryn. *Mamma's Bank Account*. New York, Harcourt, Brace, 1949. $1.45 (paperback). A very human story, honestly sentimental, about a Norwegian family in San Francisco with strong traits of courage and honesty.

Gann, Ernest. *Fiddler's Green*. New York, Sloane, 1950. o.p. An action novel; a good picture of waterfront life but one which received mixed reviews in terms of its worth as a work of literature.

———. *Of Good and Evil*. New York, Simon & Shuster, 1963. Perhaps not a novel at all—an absorbing and compassionate record of the passing parade of criminals in the corridors of the Hall of Justice on a single day of the year.

Hammett, Dashiell. *Novels of Dashiell Hammett*. New York, Knopf, 1965. $6.95. Hammett was an ex-Pinkerton detective and one of the major "tough guy" writers of the '20's and '30's.

Hulme, Katheryn. *We Lived As Children*. New York, Knopf, 1938. o.p. Again, family life in San Francisco but this time the viewpoint is that of children in a broken home. Well written, gentle, humorous; by the author of *Nun's Story*.

Kerouac, Jack. *The Subterraneans*. New York, Grove, 1958. o.p. The spokesman for the Beatniks with his most San Francisco stream-of-consciousness.

Lamott, Kenneth. *The Bastille Day Parade*. New York, David McKay, 1967. $4.95. A novel of demonstrations and confrontations—and with some fresh ideas, but flawed by weak characterizations.

Lee, C. Y. *The Flower Drum Song*. New York, Farrar, Straus & Giroux, 1957. o.p. A great hit as a book and movie, it is now a regular on the TV late-shows. An amusing and pathetic story of "the generation gap" in Chinatown.

Lee, Virginia. *The House That Tai Ming Built*. New York, Macmillan, 1963. $4.95. A Chinatown story of mixed-marriage.

Lewis, Oscar. *I Remember Christine*. New York, Knopf, 1942. o.p. A very well thought of novel, applauded for its ironic, satirical style and its engrossing characterization of protagonist Christine.

London, Jack. *Martin Eden*. New York, Macmillan, 1957. $5.95. First published in 1909, this novel is autobiographical, about a sailor-writer's problems. Early anti-Establishmentarianism.

Norris, Frank. *McTeague*. New York. Fawcett, 1964. $.75 (paperback). First published in 1899, this brutally realistic novel was decades ahead of its time. Still powerful, the story of the animalistic dentist of Polk Street is, perhaps, the one classic novel of San Francisco.

Slonim, Ruth. *San Francisco, "The City," in Verse*. Pullman, Wash., Washington State University Press, 1965. o.p. An interesting contrast to Coolbrith. Verse impressions of the city, dedicated to "the human clue."

Stevens, Will. *Three Street*. Garden City, New York, Doubleday, 1962. o.p. A moderately successful novel of Third Street—South of Market—by an *Examiner* journalist.

Wells, Evelyn. *City For St. Francis*. Garden City, New York, Doubleday, 1967. $5.95. A novel of the founding rather than of the city. The Anza expedition in the tradition of A. B. Guthrie's *Big Sky*.

———. *The Gentle Kingdom of Giacamo*. Garden City, New York, Doubleday, 1953. o.p. Reviewers were more fascinated by the setting—not so much San Francisco as the flower-growing fields—than by the plot or characterization.

White, Stewart Edward. *The Gray Dawn*. Garden City, New York, Doubleday, 1915. o.p. Once, White seemed to be on his way to becoming a second Jack London. This was one of his most popular books, part of a trilogy which appeared in a 1960 reprint (also o.p.) as *The Story of California*. Very good local color for an historical novel; vivid recreation of the Vigilante days, a la Bret Harte. Lacking unity, the parts are better than the whole. Perhaps overly genteel and romanticized.

Index

This book was printed and bound by Graphic Arts Center, using lithograph film made by Balzer-Shopes, San Francisco. Body type is Times Roman, composed by Holmes Typography, Inc., San Jose, California; type for heads is Trooper Roman, composed by Continental Graphics, Los Angeles.